OXFORD ST

Series Editor: Steven Croft

Literature of the First World War

Edited by Helen Cross

Oxford University Press

OXFORD
UNIVERSITY PRESS

Great Clarendon Street, Oxford OX2 6DP

Oxford University Press is a department of the University of Oxford.
It furthers the University's objective of excellence in research, scholarship,
and education by publishing worldwide in

Oxford   New York

Auckland   Cape Town   Dar es Salaam   Hong Kong   Karachi
Kuala Lumpur   Madrid   Melbourne   Mexico City   Nairobi
New Delhi   Shanghai   Taipei   Toronto

With offices in

Argentina   Austria   Brazil   Chile   Czech Republic   France   Greece
Guatemala   Hungary   Italy   Japan   South Korea   Poland   Portugal
Singapore   Switzerland   Thailand   Turkey   Ukraine   Vietnam

Oxford is a registered trade mark of Oxford University Press
in the UK and in certain other countries

© Helen Cross 2011

The moral rights of the author have been asserted

Database right Oxford University Press (maker)

First published 2011

All rights reserved. No part of this publication may be reproduced,
stored in a retrieval system, or transmitted, in any form or by any means,
without the prior permission in writing of Oxford University Press,
or as expressly permitted by law, or under terms agreed with the appropriate
reprographics rights organization. Enquiries concerning reproduction
outside the scope of the above should be sent to the Rights Department,
Oxford University Press, at the address above

You must not circulate this book in any other binding or cover
and you must impose this same condition on any acquirer

British Library Cataloguing in Publication Data

Data available

ISBN: 978-0-19-8310754

1 3 5 7 9 10 8 6 4 2

Typeset in India by TNQ Books and Journals Pvt. Ltd.

Printed in China by Printplus

Paper used in the production of this book is a natural, recyclable product made from
wood grown in sustainable forests. The manufacturing process conforms to the environ-
mental regulations of the country of origin.

The publishers would like to thank the following for permission to reproduce photographs:

Page 3: Imperial War Museum; page 5: Imperial War Museum; page 9: Hulton-Deutsch
Collection/Corbis; page 145: Hulton-Deutsch Collection/Corbis; page 152: The Art
Archive/Alamy; page 155: Imperial War Museum; page 161: Imperial War Museum;
page 171: Imperial War Museum; page 175: Imperial War Museum;
page 180: Hulton Archive/Getty Images.

Contents

Acknowledgements vi

Foreword viii

The First World War in Context 1
The world at war 1
Changing attitudes 4
The war in literature 7
Time perspectives 8

Literature of the First World War 13

Outbreak of War 15
The Vigil: Henry Newbolt 15
Chronicle of Youth (Great War Diary 1913–1917): Vera Brittain 16
Song of the Soldiers (Men Who March Away): Thomas Hardy 19
The Call: R.E. Vernède 21
On Receiving News of the War: Isaac Rosenberg 22

Conflict Begins 24
War and Literature: Edmund Gosse 24
Give Us Men!: The Bishop of Exeter 25
The Dead (Sonnet 3): Rupert Brooke 25
A Subaltern on the Somme: Max Plowman 26

The 'Enemy' 29
Christmas 1914: Frederick Chandler 29
To Germany: Charles Hamilton Sorley 30
Letter to Vera Brittain: Roland Leighton 31
A Dead Boche: Robert Graves 32

Under Fire 33
France at War: Rudyard Kipling 33

The Attack: R.H. Tawney   36
In Parenthesis: David Jones   41
Under Fire: Henri Barbusse   44
Letter to Susan Owen: Wilfred Owen   48
Outline: Paul Nash   50
Counter-Attack: Siegfried Sassoon   52
Dreamers: Siegfried Sassoon   53
Exposure: Wilfred Owen   54
The Show: Wilfred Owen   55

Casualties of War   58
Non-Combatants and Others: Rose Macaulay   58
Journey's End: R.C. Sherriff   61
The New Book of Martyrs: Georges Duhamel   63
Disabled: Wilfred Owen   66

Non-Combatants   69
My Heart's Right There: Florence L. Barclay   69
Non-Combatant: Cicely Hamilton   72
A Journal of Impressions in Belgium: May Sinclair   73
Mr Britling Sees It Through: H.G. Wells   76

Armistice   80
'And There Was a Great Calm': Thomas Hardy   80
Testament of Youth: Vera Brittain   82
Now It Can Be Told: Philip Gibbs   85

Later Perspectives on the War   87
Parade's End: Ford Madox Ford   87
Oh What a Lovely War: Theatre Workshop   90
MCMXIV: Philip Larkin   92
Strange Meeting: Susan Hill   93
Observe the Sons of Ulster Marching Towards the Somme:
   Frank McGuinness   97
Waiting for the Telegram: Alan Bennett   100

Notes 103

Interpretations 137
Language, style and attitude 137
  'Clarion call' 137
  Disillusionment 143
  Describing the indescribable 146
  Close-ups and distance shots 150
Conflicts and contrasts 153
  Them and us 153
  Combatants and non-combatants 156
  Officers and men 157
  War and nature 160
  Heroes and cowards 164
  Men and women 173
Aftermath 178

Essay Questions 183

Chronology 187

Further Reading 198

Acknowledgements

We gratefully acknowledge permission to use the following copyright texts in this book.

Extracts from the *Authorized Version of the Bible* (*The King James Bible*), the rights in which are vested in the Crown, are reproduced by permission of the Crown's Patentee, Cambridge University Press.

Henri Barbusse translated by Robin Buss: extract from *Under Fire* (Penguin Classics, 2003), translation copyright © Robin Buss 2003, reprinted by permission of Penguin Books Ltd.

Alan Bennett: extract from 'Waiting for the Telegram' in *Talking Heads* (BBC, 2007), reprinted by permission of The Random House Group Ltd.

Laurence Binyon: lines from 'To Women' from *The Cause: Poems of the War* (Houghton Mifflin, 1917), reprinted by permission of The Society of Authors as the Literary Representative of the Estate of Laurence Binyon.

Vera Brittain: extracts from *Testament of Youth* (Victor Gollancz, 1933) and *Chronicle of Youth: Great War Diary 1913–1917* (Victor Gollancz, 1981), reprinted by permission of Mark Bostridge and Timothy Brittain-Catlin, literary executors for the Vera Brittain Estate, 1970.

Frederick Chandler: Letter (Christmas 1914) from *Meetings in No Man's Land: Christmas 1914 and Fraternization in the Great War* edited by Marc Ferro, Malcolm Brown, Remy Cazals and Olaf Mueller (Constable, 2007), reprinted by permission of Sir Geoffrey Chandler.

Georges Duhamel translated by Florence Simmonds: extract from *The New Book of Martyrs* (Heinemann, 1918); copyright holder not traced.

Philip Gibbs: extract from 'For What Men Died' in *Now It Can be Told* (Harper & Bros, 1920); copyright holder not traced.

Robert Graves: 'A Dead Boche' from *Fairies and Fusiliers* (Heinemann, 1918) and from *The Complete Poems in One Volume* (Carcanet, 2000), reprinted by permission of Carcanet Press Ltd.

Cicely Hamilton: 'Non-Combatant' first published in *The Westminster Gazette* from *Poems of the Great War* edited by J.W. Cunliffe (Macmillan, 1916); copyright holder not traced.

Susan Hill: extract from *Strange Meeting* (Hamish Hamilton, 1971), copyright © Susan Hill 1971, 1989, reprinted by permission of Sheil Land Associates Ltd.

David Jones: extracts from *In Parenthesis* (Faber, 1937), reprinted by permission of Faber & Faber Ltd.

Philip Larkin: 'MCMXIV' from *The Whitsun Weddings* (Faber, 1964), reprinted by permission of Faber & Faber Ltd.

Roland Leighton: Letter to Vera Brittain from *Letters from a Lost Generation: First World War letters of Vera Brittain and four friends*, edited by Alan Bishop and Mark Bostridge (Little Brown, 1998); copyright holder not traced.

Rose Macaulay: extract from *Non-Combatants and Others* (Hodder & Stoughton, 1916/Capuchin Classics, 2010), reprinted by permission of the present publishers, Stacey International.

Frank McGuinness: extract from *Observe the Sons of Ulster Marching* (Faber, 1986), reprinted by permission of Faber & Faber Ltd.

Paul Nash: extracts from *Outline* (Faber, 1949); copyright holder not traced.

Wilfred Owen: Letter 48, Friday 19 January 1917 from *Collected Letters* edited by Harold Owen and John Bell (OUP, 1967), reprinted by permission of Oxford University Press.

Max Plowman: extract from *A Subaltern on the Somme* (J.M. Dent & Sons, 1928), reprinted by permission of Greta Plowman.

Siegfried Sassoon: 'Dreamers' and 'Counter-Attack' from *The Counter-Attack and Other Poems* (E.P. Dutton, 1918), and statement about the war published in *The Times* 31 July 1919, copyright © Siegfried Sassoon, reprinted by permission of the Estate of George Sassoon c/o Barbara Levy Literary Agency.

R.C. Sherriff: extract from *Journey's End* (Victor Gollancz, 1929), copyright © R.C. Sherriff 1929, reprinted by permission of Curtis Brown Group Ltd, London on behalf of the Estate of R.C. Sherriff.

May Sinclair: extract from *A Journal of Impressions in Belgium (August 1915)* (Macmillan, 1915); copyright holder not traced.

R.H. Tawney: extracts from 'The Attack' first published in *The Westminster Gazette*, from *The Attack and Other Papers* (Allen & Unwin, 1952); copyright holder not traced.

Theatre Workshop: extract from *Oh What a Lovely War* (Methuen, 1965), copyright © Joan Littlewood Productions, reprinted by permission of The Sayle Literary Agency; lyrics of the songs contained in the extract reprinted by permission of EMI Music Publishing and TRO Essex Music Ltd.

H.G. Wells: extract from *Mr Britling Sees It Through* (P.F. Collier & Sons, 1916), reprinted by permission of A.P. Watt Ltd on behalf of the Literary Executors of the Estate of H.G. Wells.

We have made every effort to trace and contact copyright holders before publication. If notified, the publisher will rectify any errors or omissions at the earliest opportunity.

Acknowledgements from Helen Cross

With many thanks, as always, to Jan Doorly, for her careful and thoughtful editing, and to Steven Croft for his supportive feedback and helpful suggestions. I would like to dedicate this volume to the memory of my grandfather, Edwin Hoyle, artist, of the Argyll and Sutherland Highlanders, who fought on the Western Front but never spoke of it.

Editors

Steven Croft, the series editor, holds degrees from Leeds and Sheffield universities. He has taught at secondary and tertiary level and headed the Department of English and Humanities in a tertiary college. He has 25 years' examining experience at A level and is currently a Principal Examiner for English. He has written several books on teaching English at A level, and his publications for Oxford University Press include *Exploring Literature*, *Success in AQA Language and Literature* and *Exploring Language and Literature*.

Helen Cross read English Literature and Music at the University of Glasgow and later was awarded an MA in Life Writing (with distinction) at the University of York. Over the past 20 years she has taught English and English Literature in comprehensive schools and in the private sector. She is an Associate Lecturer for the Open University and has been an examiner in A level English Literature. She has edited *Wilfred Owen: Selected Poems and Letters* in this series, and with Steven Croft she is joint author of A level English Literature textbooks published by Oxford University Press including *Exploring Literature* and *Success in Literature*.

Foreword

Oxford Student Texts have, over a number of years, established a reputation for presenting literary texts to students in both a scholarly and an accessible way. In response to developments in the structure and approach of A level study, several new editions have been published to help students prepare for the changing emphasis and demands of these courses. These editions have been written with a key focus on a specific area of study and contain a range of texts by a wide variety of writers intended to give a flavour of that area and provide contextual linking material that will help students develop their wider reading on a particular period or topic. Each volume in the series consists of four main sections which link together to provide an integrated approach.

The first part provides important background information about the period or thematic area and the factors that played an important part in shaping literary works. This discussion sets the various texts in context and explores some key contextual factors.

This section is followed by the texts themselves. The texts are presented without accompanying notes so that students can engage with them on their own terms without the influence of secondary ideas. To encourage this approach, the Notes are placed in the third section, immediately following the texts. The Notes provide a brief explanation of individual texts to help set them in context and also give explanations of particular words, phrases, images, allusions and so forth, to help students gain a full understanding of the particular text. They also raise questions or highlight particular issues or ideas which are important to consider when arriving at interpretations.

The fourth section, Interpretations, goes on to discuss a range of issues in more detail. This involves an examination of the influence of contextual factors as well as looking at such aspects as language and style, and various critical views or interpretations. A range of activities for students to carry out, together with discussions as to how these might be approached, are integrated into this section.

At the end of each volume there is a selection of Essay Questions, a Further Reading list and a Chronology.

We hope you enjoy reading these texts and working with these supporting materials, and wish you every success in your studies.

Steven Croft   *Series Editor*

The First World War in Context

The world at war

> [T]he First World War remains a powerful imaginative force, perhaps the most powerful force, in the shaping not only of our conceptions of what war is, but of the world we live in – a world in which that war, and all the wars that have followed it, were possible human acts. Our world begins with that war.
> (Samuel Hynes, *A War Imagined: The First World War and English Culture*, 1990, page 469)

The 'Great War' of 1914–1918 was one of the greatest catastrophes of modern times. Its impact was immense and far-reaching. This so-called 'war to end wars' achieved nothing of the kind, but it did bring about profound changes in society, culture and ways of thinking. It is said to have marked the true beginning of the 'modern age'. It also seems to have taken on a special, almost mythical, significance. The stark wastelands of mud and shattered trees, tin-hatted soldiers, barbed wire and poppies of the First World War have become iconic images of war, and remain so even for those born many decades later.

The First World War is sometimes described as a journey from innocence to experience. Although the common view of the years before the war as an idyllic 'lull before the storm' is rather exaggerated – there was an escalating threat of civil war in Ireland, for example – it is true to say that at the beginning of the twentieth century, in the years leading up to the war, many people held a simpler view of life and history than we do today. This was underpinned by the belief that human civilization was perpetually advancing, and that progress was always in the direction of what was finer or greater. Traditional moral values seemed safe and reliable; unquestioning faith in religion and in political leaders was much more common; the hierarchical British social class system was firmly entrenched and, despite the protests of the Suffragettes, conventional gender roles had hardly been challenged. All of these

The First World War in Context

aspects of society were to be thrown into disarray by a war that was shockingly different from anything that had been known before. By the time the war ended, Thomas Hardy suggests, *old hopes that earth was bettering slowly/ Were dead and damned* (see page 81).

The war was sparked when Archduke Franz Ferdinand, heir to the throne of Austro-Hungary, was murdered by a Serbian patriot. This relatively insignificant incident ignited long-standing tensions between the European nations. Rivalries had developed over territories in Africa and the Middle East, leading to a competitive expansion of armed forces in France, Germany and Britain. Once conflict began, it was not long before most of Europe was involved, owing to a system of treaties that required nations to support their allies. Russia supported the Serbians, France had a treaty with Russia, and Britain had one with France. These became known as the 'Allied Powers'. Germany supported Austria, and they were joined by Turkey, to form the 'Central Powers'.

It was by far the most enormous armed conflict that had ever taken place and became truly a world war. The fighting extended to Russia, Africa, Turkey, Palestine and the Persian Gulf, as well as both the Atlantic and Pacific Oceans, and America also entered the fray in 1917. The number of casualties was staggering: more than 37 million people were killed or wounded.

At the same time, the war was conducted in ways that had been previously unknown. In the past, wars had usually been fought by professional armies who engaged in battles at a distance from civilian life, but now there was 'total war': all the resources of each nation, at home and abroad, were focused on the war effort. All eligible males were initially encouraged and later conscripted to fight, and women's lives were drastically affected too. Although they did not participate directly in combat, some women experienced the war at close quarters, serving as army nurses or in the Women's Auxiliary Army Corps. Many more lost husbands, lovers and potential future partners. On the home front, as more and more men went to fight, gender divisions became less rigid as women filled gaps in the workforce and took on roles that had never been open to them before.

The world at war

Advances in technology also changed the face of warfare. Machine guns, tanks, poison gas and new and deadly types of bombs and shells were all used for the first time. At the beginning of the war, soldiers were still trained to fight face-to-face, with bayonets, but this kind of individual combat was soon superseded. Mechanized weapons, which killed impersonally and indiscriminately, became the order of the day. Literally and psychologically, it became easier to kill. At sea, submarines became more deadly and more widely used, while the first ever air raids, from Zeppelin airships, killed civilians and brought war much closer to home (see, for example, the extract from H.G. Wells on page 76).

A major feature of the First World War was the notorious trench system. Along the battlefronts, each side dug deep ditches, which were lined with sandbags and duckboards and protected by parapets and barbed-wire entanglements. At intervals there were 'dugouts': deeper holes in which men lived, sometimes for months at a time, in atrocious conditions. Between the opposing

Trenches on the Western Front, 1918

lines lay 'No Man's Land', sometimes no more than 50 feet wide. The system was meant to protect soldiers and equipment, and provide a base from which they could go 'over-the-top' to launch an attack. However, much of the Western Front in Belgium and Northern France was only just above sea-level, and bad weather and shelling often reduced the trenches to a rat-infested swamp, littered with the festering remains of thousands of corpses. The trench system made possible a 'war of attrition' in which each side tried to wear down the other, and fighting dragged on in what sometimes seemed an interminable stalemate.

Changing attitudes

In August 1914, when Britain joined the conflict, many people were filled with a patriotic fervour and idealism which, with hindsight, seems painfully naïve and out of tune with the real reasons for the war. It was a hundred years since Britain had been directly involved in a major war and no one had any real experience of what war was like. According to A.J.P. Taylor in *The First World War* (1963), 'All imagined that it would be an affair of great marches and great battles, quickly decided' (page 158).

Young men, susceptible to propaganda that presented the war in old-fashioned terms, as a moral battle against an evil power, signed up willingly. Dying for their country was regarded as an honour, or a religious duty, that would win them 'glory'. Rupert Brooke captured the mood in his sequence of sonnets, *1914* (see page 25):

> Now, God be thanked Who has matched us with His hour,
> And caught our youth, and wakened us from sleeping,
> With hand made sure, clear eye, and sharpened power

Recruiting campaigns offered these young men the opportunity to prove their 'sporting spirit' and earn the respect of future generations.

Changing attitudes

Recruiting posters such as this encouraged young men to regard it as their duty to sign up

Although some people were against the war from the start, their views tended to be drowned out by propaganda or silenced by censorship. However, as the war – which was meant to be 'all over by Christmas', in a popular phrase – dragged on, and casualty lists became longer, the questioning increased. By the end of 1915, some were beginning to ask: 'What have we been fighting for? What are we fighting for? Do you know? Does anyone know?' (H.G. Wells, *Mr Britling Sees It Through*, 1916, page 303; see page 76).

From mid-1916 onwards, attitudes to the war changed more and more. The Battle of the Somme, which raged over the summer, is regarded as the turning point. The Allies launched a huge offensive in the area of the River Somme on 1 July, but planning and preparation were poor and the strength of the German defences had been underestimated. Very little was achieved. There were 60,000 British casualties on the first day

The First World War in Context

alone, and more than a million lives were lost overall. People began to question whether slaughter on this scale was worthwhile. (See R.H. Tawney's comments in *The Attack* on page 36, for example.)

For the remainder of the war, critical and dissenting voices became more and more prominent. Many held the view that the government, the generals and powerful business interests were combining to prolong the war unnecessarily, and were indifferent to the fate of the men in the trenches. For example, the poet and author Siegfried Sassoon (see pages 52–53 and 118), who had fought on the Somme and been awarded the Military Cross for 'conspicuous gallantry', came to believe that the government could have ended the war by diplomacy but had chosen not to for political reasons, and thus sacrificed the lives of thousands of men. He threw away his medal and denounced the war in a famous public statement of July 1917: 'I am a soldier, convinced that I am acting on behalf of soldiers. I believe that the war upon which I entered as a war of defence and liberation has now become a war of aggression and conquest.'

In the same statement Sassoon also criticized the civilian population for their 'callous complacency' and apparent indifference to the suffering of the soldiers. Although his protest was suppressed and he was sent to a mental institution – he was considered 'a lunatic' by the War Office, according to confidential army files released in 1998 – it is clear that by the mid-point of the war, many soldiers on both sides felt that the war was being deliberately and needlessly prolonged.

Many more months of stalemate ensued; the Germans launched a huge 'Spring Offensive' early in 1918; but eventually, with the added weight of the Americans, who had joined the war in April 1917, the Allies were able to break through and advance to victory, though not without heavy losses. The war finally ended with the signing of the Armistice at 11 am on 11 November 1918.

Although the ending of the war came as a relief for many, and there were celebrations and dancing in the streets, for others the world had been changed beyond recognition and their reactions were much more ambivalent. Thomas Gowenlock, an American intelligence officer, recorded afterwards that for soldiers at the Front, the war had become so much a way of life that the 'abrupt release from it all was physical and psychological agony'. Many could not believe that the war was over, or relate to anything else:

> What was to come next? They did not know – and hardly cared. Their minds were numbed by the shock of peace. The past consumed their whole consciousness. The present did not exist – and the future was inconceivable.
> (Thomas Gowenlock, *Soldiers of Darkness*, 1936)

The war in literature

The First World War was a very *literary* war. In the days before electronic mass media, the written word was vital for communication, and an enormous event like the war inevitably prompted a great outpouring of writing in all its forms. In the public sphere, when war was declared the British government rapidly set up various agencies to promote its message on the war, and eventually brought these together in a Ministry of Information, which might equally well have been named the Ministry of Propaganda. Many well-known writers were summoned and asked to contribute to the war effort by writing to influence public opinion in favour of the war. They produced poems, essays and journalistic pieces which were circulated in the daily newspapers. Large numbers of novels were also written during the war, but many of those were intended as 'patriotic' propaganda and were of little literary merit, like the extract by Florence Barclay on page 69. Works that were anti-war, or critical of government policy, were much less likely to be published. It was a similar story with drama: mediocre plays that supported the war and the government were staged, but anything more radical was suppressed.

On a more personal level, for those directly involved in the fighting, writing was the only means by which they could maintain contact with their loved ones. Even in the midst of battle, apparently, the post reached its destination quite rapidly. Almost every soldier corresponded regularly with those at home, generating huge numbers of letters, ranging from the standard 'field postcard' to sophisticated literary accounts; see, for example, the letter by Wilfred Owen on page 48.

Confined to trenches for long periods, often with little to do but wait, many men who might not otherwise have done so also tried their hands at poetry. While letters were subject to censorship, to avoid giving away information to the enemy or lowering morale at home, poetry was considered a 'safe' way to express the truth about the war.

However, the literary context of the First World War includes a great deal more than the enormous amount of writing produced between 1914 and 1918. It ranges from a consideration of literature written in the years leading up to the war, right up to the present day, and it is an ever-growing field as writers look back to the war through the lens of later decades.

Time perspectives

In the years immediately before the war, the work of a group known as the Georgian poets was popular. Unlike either the formal, traditional work of the Victorian writers who came before, or the challenging, experimental work of the Modernists which was beginning to develop at the same time, Georgian writing is associated with a rather old-fashioned, romantic and somewhat sentimental presentation of 'Englishness', which captures something of the spirit of the pre-war years. Some of the best-known war poets, including Siegfried Sassoon, contributed to collections of Georgian poetry before they became involved in the war. Elements of Georgian style, such as simple, traditional verse forms and natural language, are common in their work, even though the subject matter is so different.

Time perspectives

Siegfried Sassoon in 1915

The beginning of the war sparked an effusion of patriotic feeling, which was expressed in the exalted, romantic language of poets such as R.E. Vernède (see page 21) and Rupert Brooke (see page 25). Idealized images of glorious battles and the hero's death inspired many young men to enlist. With the wisdom of hindsight, we tend to view this kind of writing as poignantly naïve, or hypocritical, or ironic in the face of what was to come, but at the time the sentiments were genuine enough.

By the end of the war, this innocence was well and truly shattered, to be replaced by anger, bitterness and despair. Writers such as Wilfred Owen, Siegfried Sassoon and the many other 'trench poets' who aimed to expose the horror and pity of war tend to be the first to come to mind when we think of First World War literature. Several examples are included here in the section entitled 'Under Fire' (see pages 33–57).

In the decades following the war, many survivors struggled to find a way to live in a world that had been irrevocably altered. It has been suggested that it took around ten years before many were able to come to terms with their experience sufficiently to be able to write about it with some sense of perspective. From the mid-1920s onwards, a steady stream of memoirs and novels about the war began to appear. Memoirs by Siegfried Sassoon, Edmund Blunden and Robert Graves are among the most famous, along with Vera Brittain's *Testament of Youth* (see page 82). Novelists such as Ernest Hemingway and Ford Madox Ford (see page 87) also wrote reflectively about the war and its effects with the wider perspective of hindsight.

Only one generation later, attention was focused on the new conflict of 1939–1945. Not surprisingly, little First World War literature was produced at this time, but some writers inevitably pointed out the irony that it had been called 'the war to end wars'. However, between the 1950s and the1980s, there was renewed interest in the First World War as an 'archetypal war'. This was the era of the 'Cold War', which involved the polarization of the world between East and West, Communism and Capitalism, Russia and America. With its recurrent crises, it was a time of tension. The fear of nuclear holocaust was widespread and anti-war feeling was strong. At the same time, now that most of the survivors of the First World War were dead, it became acceptable to use the war as a subject for satire and black comedy. The musical *Oh What a Lovely War* (1963, see page 90) was highly successful at a time when people were torn between fear, protest and despair.

Since 1990, many more documents such as letters, diaries, and new biographies have been researched and published. Understanding of the psychology of war and trauma is more sophisticated, and what was once 'unspeakable' has become almost commonplace. Graphic descriptions of horrific events are less unusual than they once were, and television images of war reach our homes daily. Now that there is almost no one alive who remembers the First World War, there is more freedom to offer fictional interpretations, and contemporary novelists such as Susan Hill (see page 93), Pat Barker and Sebastian Faulks, and

Time perspectives

dramatists such as Frank McGuinness (see page 97) have returned to the subject for inspiration. Authors continue to be fascinated by all aspects of this devastating war, and to re-present it in drama, poetry and fiction.

All the texts in this selection relate in some way to the First World War as it was experienced on the Western Front in Northern Europe. It is important to remain aware that the war was a truly global catastrophe, involving people from almost every continent, fighting on many fronts. However, in a volume of this size, it is possible to include only a small selection from a wealth of interesting possibilities.

This selection provides a range of extracts and poems that explore a wide variety of themes, attitudes and viewpoints. The texts have been organized into groups, partly by time of writing and partly by theme. Combatant and non-combatant writers are represented, and the texts were produced at different times, ranging from reactions to the outbreak of war in 1914 to imaginative responses written many decades after it ended.

Literature of the First
World War

Outbreak of War

The Vigil: Henry Newbolt

England! where the sacred flame
    Burns before the inmost shrine,
Where the lips that love thy name
    Consecrate their hopes and thine,
Where the banners of thy dead
Weave their shadows overhead,
Watch beside thine arms to-night,
Pray that God defend the Right.

Think that when to-morrow comes
    War shall claim command of all,
Thou must hear the roll of drums,
    Thou must hear the trumpet's call.
Now, before thy silence ruth,
Commune with the voice of truth;
England! on thy knees to-night
Pray that God defend the Right.

Single-hearted, unafraid,
    Hither all thy heroes came,
On this altar's steps were laid
    Gordon's life and Outram's fame.
England! if thy will be yet
By their great example set,
Here beside thine arms to-night
Pray that God defend the Right.

So shalt thou when morning comes
    Rise to conquer or to fall,
Joyful hear the rolling drums,
    Joyful hear the trumpets call,
Then let Memory tell thy heart:
'England! what thou wert, thou art!'
Gird thee with thine ancient might,
Forth! and God defend the Right!

Chronicle of Youth (Great War Diary 1913–1917): Vera Brittain

Monday August 3rd 1914

To-day has been far too exciting to enable me to feel at all like sleep – in fact it is one of the most thrilling I have ever lived through, though without doubt there are many more to come. That which has been so long anticipated by some & scoffed at by others has come to pass at last – Armageddon in Europe! On Saturday evening Germany declared war upon Russia & also started advancing towards the French frontier. The French, in order to make it evident that they were not the aggressors, wasted some hours & then the order to mobilise was given. Great excitement in France continued throughout the night & yesterday the Germans attacked France without declaring war. Unconfirmed rumour says that in one place they have been repulsed with heavy losses. [...]

    I should think this must be the blackest Bank Holiday within memory. Pandemonium reigned in the town. What with holiday-trippers, people struggling for papers, trying to lay in stores of food & dismayed that the price of everything had gone up, there was confusion everywhere. Mother met Mrs Whitehead in the town; she is in great anxiety because she has one son in Russia, one – Jack – in Servia, and another on his way from India. Marjorie Briggs, who was to have been married on Saturday, was married in a hurry on Friday as her husband had to have joined his regiment on Saturday. The papers are full of stories of tourists in hopeless plights trying to get back to England. Paper money is useless & the majority of the trains are cut off. It is rumoured that there is fear in Paris that a fleet of German Zeppelins are going to destroy Paris from above in the night.

Tuesday August 4th

Late as it is & almost too excited to write as I am, I must make some effort to chronicle the stupendous events of this remarkable day. The situation is absolutely unparalleled in the history of the world. Never before has the war strength of each individual nation been of such great extent, even though all the nations of Europe, the dominant continent, have been armed before. It is estimated that when the war begins, *14 millions* of men will be engaged in the conflict. Attack is possible by earth, water & air, & the destruction attainable by the modern war machines used by the armies is unthinkable & past imagination. [...]

Wednesday August 5th

All the news of last night was confirmed this morning, and it is further announced that the time limit given by Britain for an answer to her ultimatum expired without a reply coming from Germany, and that war between England & Germany is formally declared. Papers seemed to differ as to whether England must be said to have made war on Germany or Germany on England. Some say that the Germans have started hostilities against us by sinking a British mining ship and chasing a British cruiser. Thus, as the papers point out, Germany has declared war on four powers – Russia, France, Belgium and Britain, within 3 days. Nothing like it, they say, has been known since the time of Napoleon, and even Napoleon did not make war on his neighbours at so mad a rate.

The town was quite quiet when we went down, though groups of people were standing about talking & one or two Territorials were passing through the streets. Several Territorials & one or two Reservists were going off by train this morning & there was a small crowd on the station seeing them off. Close by us a Reservist got into a carriage & his father & a girl, probably his wife, came to say goodbye. The girl was crying but they were all quite calm. As we came up from the town I met Maurice and went down again with him. Though excitement & suspense are wearing, I felt I simply could not rest but must go on wandering about. [...]

I showed Edward an appeal in *The Times & the Chronicle* for young unmarried men between the ages of 18 & 30 to join the army. He suddenly got very keen & after dinner he & Maurice wandered all round Buxton trying to find out what to do in order to volunteer for home service. They were informed by someone at the Police Station that the best thing to do would be to telephone to the Territorial Headquarters at Chesterfield. [...]

Thursday August 6th

To-day has principally been one of the weary waiting kind. Nothing very definite has happened. Edward & Maurice have as yet heard nothing from the adjutant at Chesterfield. Nothing very definite is known about England's policy & the papers are naturally secretive about the position of her Fleet. The chief news is that the Germans have been repulsed with heavy losses while trying to storm the Belgian fortification of Liège. The Belgians are said to have behaved magnificently & while the defenders of the forts were engaged in keeping the invaders at bay, a Belgian brigade arrived & crowned the splendid efforts of the defenders with success.

To-day I started the only work it seems possible as yet for women to do – the making of garments for the soldiers. I started knitting sleeping-helmets, and as I have forgotten how to knit, & was never very brilliant when I knew, I seemed to be an object of some amusement. But even when one is not skilful it is better to proceed slowly than to do *nothing* to help.

Song of the Soldiers (Men Who March Away): Thomas Hardy

What of the faith and fire within us
    Men who march away
    Ere the barn-cocks say
    Night is growing gray,
To hazards whence no tears can win us;
What of the faith and fire within us
    Men who march away!

Outbreak of War

Is it a purblind prank, O think you,
    Friend with the musing eye
    Who watch us stepping by,
    With doubt and dolorous sigh?
Can much pondering so hoodwink you!
Is it a purblind prank, O think you,
    Friend with the musing eye?

Nay. We see well what we are doing,
    Though some may not see –
    Dalliers as they be! –
    England's need are we;
Her distress would leave us rueing:
Nay. We see well what we are doing,
    Though some may not see!

In our heart of hearts believing
    Victory crowns the just,
    And that braggarts must
    Surely bite the dust,
Press we to the field ungrieving,
In our heart of hearts believing
    Victory crowns the just.

Hence the faith and fire within us
    Men who march away
    Ere the barn-cocks say
    Night is growing gray,
To hazards whence no tears can win us;
Hence the faith and fire within us
    Men who march away.

The Call: R.E. Vernède

Lad, with the merry smile and the eyes
    Quick as a hawk's and clear as the day,
You, who have counted the game the prize,
    Here is the game of games to play.
    Never a goal – the captains say – 5
Matches the one that's needed now:
    Put the old blazer and cap away –
England's colours await your brow.

Man, with the square-set jaws and chin,
    Always, it seems, you have moved to your end 10
Sure of yourself, intent to win
    Fame and wealth and the power to bend –
    All that you've made you're called to spend,
All that you've sought you're asked to miss –
    What's ambition compared with this 15
That a man lay down his life for his friend?

Dreamer, oft in your glancing mind
    Brave with drinking the faerie brew,
You have smitten the ogres blind
    When the fair Princess cried out to you. 20
    Dreamer, what if your dreams are true?
Yonder's a bayonet, magical, since
    Him whom it strikes, the blade sinks through –
Take it and strike for England, Prince!

Friend with the face so hard and worn, 25
    The Devil and you have sometime met,
And now you curse the day you were born,
    And want one boon of God – to forget.

Outbreak of War

      Ah, but I know, and yet – and yet –
I think, out there in the shrapnel spray,
      You shall stand up and not regret
The Life that gave so splendid a day.

Lover of ease, you've lolled and forgot
      All the things that you meant to right;
Life has been soft for you, has it not?
      What offer does England make to-night?
      This – to toil and to march and to fight
As never you've dreamed since your life began;
      This – to carry the steel-swept height,
This – to know that you've played the man!

Brothers, brothers, the time is short,
      Nor soon again shall it so betide
That a man may pass from the common sort
      Sudden and stand by the heroes' side.
      Are there some that being named yet bide? –
Hark once more to the clarion call –
      Sounded by him who deathless died –
'This day England expects you all.'

On Receiving News of the War: Isaac Rosenberg

Snow is a strange white word.
No ice or frost
Have asked of bud or bird
For Winter's cost.

Yet ice and frost and snow
From earth to sky
This Summer land doth know.
No man knows why.

In all men's hearts it is.
Some spirit old
Hath turned with malign kiss
Our lives to mould.

Red fangs have torn His face.
God's blood is shed.
He mourns from His lone place
His children dead.

O! ancient crimson curse!
Corrode, consume.
Give back this universe
Its pristine bloom.

Conflict Begins

War and Literature: Edmund Gosse

War is the great scavenger of thought. It is the sovereign disinfectant, and its red stream of blood is the Condy's Fluid that cleans out the stagnant pools and clotted channels of the intellect. I suppose that hardly any Englishman who is capable of a renovation of the mind has failed to feel during the last few weeks a certain solemn refreshment of the spirit, a humble and mournful consciousness that his ideals, his aims, his hopes during our late past years of luxury and peace have been founded on a misconception of our aims as a nation, of our right to possess a leading place in the sunlighted spaces of the world. We have awakened from an opium-dream of comfort, of ease, of that miserable poltroonery of 'the sheltered life.' Our wish for indulgence of every sort, our laxity of manners, our wretched sensitiveness to personal inconvenience, these are suddenly lifted before us in their true guise as the spectres of national decay; and we have risen from the lethargy of our dilettantism to lay them, before it is too late, by the flashing of the unsheathed sword. 'Slaughter is God's daughter,' a poet said a hundred years ago, and that strange phrase of Coleridge's, which has been so often ridiculed by a slothful generation, takes a new and solemn significance to ears and eyes awakened at last by the strong red glare of reality.

Give Us Men!: The Bishop of Exeter

Give us Men!
    Men – from every rank,
    Fresh and free and frank;
Men of thought and reading,
Men of light and leading,   5
Men of loyal breeding,
The Nation's welfare speeding:
Men of faith and not of fiction,
Men of lofty aim and action:
    Give us Men – I say again,   10
    Give us Men!

    Give us Men!
Men who, when the tempest gathers,
Grasp the Standard of their fathers
    In the thickest fight: 15
Men who strike for home and altar,
(Let the coward cringe and falter,)
    God defend the right!
True as truth though lorn and lonely,
Tender, as the brave are only;   20
Men who tread where saints have trod,
Men for Country – Home – and God:
    Give us Men! I say again – again –
    Give us such Men!

The Dead (Sonnet 3): Rupert Brooke

Blow out, you bugles, over the rich Dead!
    There's none of these so lonely and poor of old,
    But, dying, has made us rarer gifts than gold.

These laid the world away; poured out the red
Sweet wine of youth; gave up the years to be
    Of work and joy, and that unhoped serene,
    That men call age; and those who would have been,
Their sons, they gave, their immortality.

Blow, bugles, blow! They brought us, for our dearth,
    Holiness, lacked so long, and Love, and Pain.
Honour has come back, as a king, to earth,
    And paid his subjects with a royal wage;
And Nobleness walks in our ways again;
    And we have come into our heritage.

A Subaltern on the Somme: Max Plowman

Charing Cross

Charing Cross Station: a sombre, sunless place, crowded with khaki figures thinly interspersed with civilians, mostly women, dressed in sombre colours. The figures in plain khaki are listless, but those decorated with ribbons, and still more those with red or blue tabs, look animated with the bustle of busy self-importance. To-day the heavy lugubrious atmosphere that often seems to pervade a London terminus is lightning-charged, so that the air vibrates with repressed emotions, felt all the more intensely because no one gives them relief. The hopes and fears of all are the same; but they are not shared: each one bears his own.

Beyond the barrier lie the trains: long black sleeping snakes. We disregard them, as if they were not. They are public servants that have become our masters. We turn away from them because we know that in this scene they are the chief instruments of destiny.

I am hideously self-conscious. One half of me is tunic, belt, puttees, badges, revolver – a figure hoping it presents an approved appearance in the public eye and faintly flattered by the sense of voluntary heroism; the other is a mind seething. This mind has become like a cloud brooding above my body, so full of violence and revolt that constant effort is required to keep it suppressed. Its impulses suggest the maddest actions. Now, as my young wife and I weave an outwardly nonchalant way through the crowd (she does not touch my arm: we know the etiquette), I am on the point of proposing that we walk straight out of the station, get into a taxi and drive and drive and drive till the car breaks down. Even the thought brings a sense of relief, for it opens a vista upon a garden of old enchantment. I draw a shutter across it violently. We go upstairs and drink coffee in the gloomy buffet.

One glance round to see there are no officers of one's own regiment here, then heart's ease for a moment. We can smile to one another. We do not speak. There is nothing to say now. Twenty-two months ago we saw this hour. We were reading *The Globe* after a little dinner at a place near the Marble Arch. We looked up, and as our eyes met we saw this day. That was a lifetime ago; but from that hour every step has been towards this chasm. Then, the rumble of earthquake bringing foreknowledge as clearly as if the red printed page had announced it: now the event, so many times lived in imagination it is difficult to realise it as fact. We look in each other's eyes to reassure one another of reality. The look implies: 'You are you. I am I. Nothing else matters.'

For all the months of grace between then and now we are not ungrateful. We have reason to give thanks. Love's embodiment now lives. I listened to the flutter of his heart as he lay on my arm last night. Kind was the fate that had kept me from going sooner; for had it been otherwise one victory over death might have been lost. We are free from double dread. For that my heart sings a song often to be sung again in strange places.

We must go. Back through the khaki whirlpool: up the long platform. Ah! There's Brunning the South African, and Zenu the bright, blond beauty, and Leonard the weed, and some more. [...]

There is something like a dozen of us in this odd saloon-car with its large, broad windows. We take our places like guests at a conference.

Now the last fierce moment comes. 'Step inside, please.' Your hand. 'Good-bye. Might be back in a fortnight: you never know. Good-bye. Never good-bye.' The train moving: a girlish figure running beyond the end of the platform waving, all sadness gone, still waving... Snap! The cord is broken. Back through the window, and here's this collection sitting round like the figures in the poem, 'all silent and all...' Well, you never know. Some will come back: some won't.

The 'Enemy'

Christmas 1914: Frederick Chandler

Before getting into the trench I came across a couple of German boots sticking out of the side of the road; attached to the boots were a couple of German legs. I called attention to the legs, and investigation showed the rest of the gentleman imperfectly covered with earth; so he was propped into a more comfortable grave – a proceeding which delights the heart of every true British soldier. Some buttons were removed to remember him by, and he was snugly covered with earth and patted down. 'Rest in peace, poor Fritz!' thought I. 'It is not you or your like who have caused this; there is not a combatant soldier in any of the combatant armies who would not make peace tomorrow; you have died bravely; and instead of Christmas in the warmth of the home you love, with your lager beer, your pipe, and your buxom haus-frau, and perhaps your little children, you lie stiff and cold with your feet sticking out of the roadside – this wretched, bullet-swept, shell-scarred roadside.' I had no feeling of hatred in my heart at this time; later I was to see the effects of German asphyxiating gas, and this changed everything; but even now I have a slightly tender corner in my heart for the Saxons, and these were Saxons opposite us now. [...]

  Many shots were exchanged that morning, but as the afternoon approached a most amazing thing occurred. All firing ceased and shouts were exchanged. Then came a tentative scrambling of a few men over the parapet,

The 'Enemy'

and a few Germans over theirs; then a scramble of dozens, then of scores of men of both sides; all met in the middle and talked and stared and exchanged cap comforters for the grey German trench cap, and bully beef for cigars. A German officer came out with an orderly with beer and glasses, little S__, our baby subaltern, was presented with a box of cigars. Two barrels of beer were rolled over to the regiment on our left, all was good fellowship and a pathetic friendliness. As dusk came on, and it came early, the men had to be called in. Shrill whistle blasts were heard everywhere and the land of death between the trenches was again deserted, and save for the grim barbed wire entanglements nothing but hard frozen mud and ice. But the men had made a compact. Not a single shot was fired, and that evening was one of the most beautiful, clear, starry, frosty nights that ever I saw, and there reigned a delectable entrancing quiet, the first quiet I had heard for months. Musical instruments were played and songs and carols were sung on both sides and Christmas dinners eaten.

To Germany: Charles Hamilton Sorley

You are blind like us. Your hurt no man designed,
And no man claimed the conquest of your land.
But gropers both through fields of thought confined
We stumble and we do not understand.
You only saw your future bigly planned,
And we, the tapering paths of our own mind,
And in each other's dearest ways we stand,
And hiss and hate. And the blind fight the blind.

When it is peace, then we may view again
With new-won eyes each other's truer form
And wonder. Grown more loving-kind and warm
We'll grasp firm hands and laugh at the old pain,
When it is peace. But until peace, the storm
The darkness and the thunder and the rain.

Letter to Vera Brittain: Roland Leighton

France, 11 September 1915

I have been rushing around since 4 a.m. this morning superintending the building of dug-outs, drawing up plans for the draining of trenches, doing a little digging myself as a relaxation, and accidentally coming upon dead Germans while looting timber from what was once a German fire trench. This latter was captured by the French not so long ago and is pitted with shell holes each big enough to bury a horse or two in. The dug-outs have been nearly all blown in, the wire entanglements are a wreck, and in among this chaos of twisted iron and splintered timber and shapeless earth are the fleshless, blackened bones of simple men who poured out their red, sweet wine of youth unknowing, for nothing more tangible than Honour or their Country's Glory or another's Lust [for] Power. Let him who thinks that War is a glorious thing, who loves to roll forth stirring words of exhortation, invoking Honour and Praise and Valour and Love of Country with as thoughtless and fervid a faith as inspired the priests of Baal to call on their own slumbering deity, let him but look at a little pile of sodden grey rags that cover half a skull and a shin bone

The 'Enemy'

and what might have been Its ribs, or at this skeleton lying on its side, resting half crouching as it fell, supported by one arm, perfect but that it is headless and with the tattered clothing still draped round it; and let him realise how grand & glorious a thing it is to have distilled all Youth and Joy and Life into a foetid heap of hideous putrescence. Who is there who has known & seen who can say that Victory is worth the death of even one of these? 25

Excuse this morbid letter, but it is my mood of the present.

And now I really must go to sleep – even although it is four in the afternoon!

A Dead Boche: Robert Graves

To you who'd read my songs of War
And only hear of blood and fame,
I'll say (you've heard it said before)
'War's Hell!' and if you doubt the same,
Today I found in Mametz Wood   5
A certain cure for lust of blood:

Where, propped against a shattered trunk,
In a great mess of things unclean,
Sat a dead Boche; he scowled and stunk
With clothes and face a sodden green,   10
Big-bellied, spectacled, crop-haired,
Dribbling black blood from nose and beard.

Under Fire

France at War: Rudyard Kipling

On the frontier of civilization

'It's a pretty park,' said the French artillery officer. 'We've done a lot for it since the owner left. I hope he'll appreciate it when he comes back.'

The car traversed a winding drive through woods, between banks embellished with little chalets of a rustic nature. At first, the chalets stood their full height above ground, suggesting tea-gardens in England. Further on they sank into the earth till, at the top of the ascent, only their solid brown roofs showed. Torn branches drooping across the driveway, with here and there a scorched patch of undergrowth, explained the reason of their modesty.

The chateau that commanded these glories of forest and park sat boldly on a terrace. There was nothing wrong with it except, if one looked closely, a few scratches or dints on its white stone walls, or a neatly drilled hole under a flight of steps. One such hole ended in an unexploded shell. 'Yes,' said the officer. 'They arrive here occasionally.'

Something bellowed across the folds of the wooded hills; something grunted in reply. Something passed overhead, querulously but not without dignity. Two clear fresh barks joined the chorus, and a man moved lazily in the direction of the guns.

'Well. Suppose we come and look at things a little,' said the commanding officer.

An observation post

There was a specimen tree – a tree worthy of such a park – the sort of tree visitors are always taken to admire. A ladder ran up it to a platform. What little wind there was swayed the tall top, and the ladder creaked like a ship's gangway. A telephone bell tinkled 50 foot overhead. Two invisible guns spoke fervently for half a minute, and broke off like terriers choked on a leash. We climbed till the topmost platform swayed sicklily beneath us. Here one found a rustic shelter, always of the tea-garden pattern, a table, a map, and a little window wreathed with living branches that gave one the first view of the Devil and all his works. It was a stretch of open country, with a few sticks like old tooth-brushes which had once been trees round a farm. The rest was yellow grass, barren to all appearance as the veldt.

'The grass is yellow because they have used gas here,' said an officer. 'Their trenches are – You can see for yourself.'

The guns in the woods began again. They seemed to have no relation to the regularly spaced bursts of smoke along a little smear in the desert earth two thousand yards away – no connection at all with the strong voices overhead coming and going. It was as impersonal as the drive of the sea along a breakwater.

Thus it went: a pause – a gathering of sound like the race of an incoming wave; then the high-flung heads of breakers spouting white up the face of a groyne. Suddenly, a seventh wave broke and spread the shape of its foam like a plume overtopping all the others.

'That's one of our torpilleurs – what you call trench-sweepers,' said the observer among the whispering leaves.

Some one crossed the platform to consult the map with its ranges. A blistering outbreak of white smokes rose a little beyond the large plume. It was as though the tide had struck a reef out yonder.

Then a new voice of tremendous volume lifted itself out of a lull that followed. Somebody laughed. Evidently the voice was known.

'That is not for us,' a gunner said. 'They are being waked up from –' he named a distant French position. 'So and so is attending to them there. We go on with our usual work. Look! Another torpilleur.'

'The barbarian'

Again a big plume rose; and again the lighter shells broke at their appointed distance beyond it. The smoke died away on that stretch of trench, as the foam of a swell dies in the angle of a harbour wall, and broke out afresh half a mile lower down. In its apparent laziness, in its awful deliberation, and its quick spasms of wrath, it was more like the work of waves than of men; and our high platform's gentle sway and glide was exactly the motion of a ship drifting with us toward that shore.

'The usual work. Only the usual work,' the officer explained. 'Sometimes it is here. Sometimes above or below us. I have been here since May.'

A little sunshine flooded the stricken landscape and made its chemical yellow look more foul. A detachment of men moved out on a road which ran toward the French trenches, and then vanished at the foot of a little rise. Other men appeared moving toward us with that concentration of purpose and bearing shown in both

Armies when – dinner is at hand. They looked like people who had been digging hard.

'The same work. Always the same work!' the officer said. 'And you could walk from here to the sea or to Switzerland in that ditch – and you'll find the same work going on everywhere. It isn't war.'

'It's better than that,' said another. 'It's the eating-up of a people. They come and they fill the trenches and they die, and they die; and they send more and *those* die. We do the same, of course, but – look!'

He pointed to the large deliberate smoke-heads renewing themselves along that yellowed beach. 'That is the frontier of civilization. They have all civilization against them – those brutes yonder. It's not the local victories of the old wars that we're after. It's the barbarian – all the barbarian. Now, you've seen the whole thing in little.'

The Attack: R.H. Tawney

The priest stood in the door of a wooden shanty. The communicants stood and knelt in ranks outside. One guessed at the familiar words through the rattling of rifle bolts, the bursts of song and occasional laughter from the other men, as they put their equipment together outside their little bivouacs, bushes bent till they met and covered with tarpaulins, or smoked happily in an unwonted freedom from fatigues. An hour later we fell in on the edge of the wood, and, after the roll was called by companies, moved off. It was a perfect evening, and the immense overwhelming tranquillity of sky and down, uniting us and millions of enemies and allies in its solemn, unavoidable embrace, dwarfed into insignificance the wrath of man and his feverish energy of destruction. One forgot the object for which we were marching to the trenches. One felt as though one were on the verge of some new and tremendous discovery; and the soft cheering of the knots of men who turned out to watch us pass seemed like the last faint hail of landsmen to explorers bound for unknown seas. Then the heat struck us, and at the first halt we flung ourselves down, panting like dogs. [...]

Some evenings before, I had watched with some friends from a peaceful little *butte* some miles behind our front the opening hours of the great bombardment. We had seen it from above, beneath a slowly sinking sun, as a long white line of surf breaking without pause on a shore that faded at its extremities into horizons beyond our sight, and had marvelled that, by some trick of the ground, not a whisper from that awe-inspiring racket reached us. Now, at the tremendous climax of the last hour of the inferno – the last, I mean, before we went over the top – another miracle was being worked.

It was a glorious morning, and, as though there were some mysterious sympathy between the wonders of the ear and of the eye, the bewildering tumult seemed to grow more insistent with the growing brilliance of the atmosphere and the intenser blue of the July sky. The sound was different, not only in magnitude, but in quality, from anything known to me. It was not a succession of explosions or a continuous roar; I, at least, never heard either a gun or a bursting shell. It was not a noise; it was a symphony. It did not move; it hung over us. It was as though the air were full of a vast and agonised passion, bursting now into groans and sighs, now into shrill screams and pitiful whimpers, shuddering beneath terrible blows, torn by unearthly whips, vibrating with the solemn pulse of enormous wings. And the supernatural tumult did not pass in this direction or that. It did not begin, intensify, decline, and end. It was poised in the air, a stationary panorama of sound, a condition of the atmosphere, not the creation of man. It seemed that one had only to lift one's eyes to be appalled by the writhing of the tormented element above one, that a hand raised ever so little above the level of the trench would be sucked away into a whirlpool revolving with cruel and incredible velocity over infinite depths. And this feeling, while it filled one with awe, filled one also with triumphant exultation, the exultation of struggling against a storm in mountains, or watching the irresistible course of a swift and destructive river. Yet at the same time one was intent on practical details, wiping the trench dirt off the bolt of one's rifle, reminding the men of what each was to do, and when the message went round, 'five minutes to go,' seeing that all bayonets were fixed. My captain, a brave man and a good officer, came along and borrowed a spare watch off me. It was the last time I saw him. At 7.30 we went up the ladders, doubled through the gaps in the wire, and lay down, waiting for the line to form up on each side of us. When it was ready we went forward, not doubling, but at a walk. For we had nine hundred yards of rough ground to the trench which was our first objective, and about fifteen hundred to a further trench where we were to wait for orders. There was a bright light in the air, and the tufts of coarse grass were grey with dew.

    I hadn't gone ten yards before I felt a load fall from me. There's a sentence at the end of *The Pilgrim's Progress* which has always struck me as one of the most awful things imagined by man: 'Then I saw that there was a way to Hell, even from the Gates of Heaven, as well as from the City of Destruction.' To have gone so far and be rejected at last! Yet undoubtedly man walks between precipices, and no one knows the rottenness in him till he cracks, and then it's too late. I had been worried by the thought: 'Suppose one should lose one's head and get other men cut up! Suppose one's legs should take fright and refuse to move!' Now I knew it was all right. I shouldn't be frightened and I shouldn't lose my head. Imagine the joy of that discovery! I felt quite happy and self-possessed. It wasn't courage. That, I imagine, is the quality of facing danger which one knows to be danger, of making one's spirit triumph over the bestial desire to live in this body. But I knew that I was in no danger. I knew I shouldn't be hurt; knew it positively, much more positively than I know most things I'm paid for knowing. I understood in a small way what Saint-Just meant when he told the soldiers who protested at his rashness that no bullet could touch the emissary of the Republic. And all the time, in spite of one's inner happiness, one was shouting the sort of thing that N.C.O.s do shout and no one attends to: 'Keep your extension'; 'Don't bunch'; 'Keep up on the left'. I remember being cursed by an orderly for yelling the same things days after in the field-hospital.

Well, we crossed three lines that had once been trenches, and tumbled into the fourth, our first objective. 'If it's all like this it's a cake-walk,' said a little man beside me, the kindest and bravest of friends, whom no weariness could discourage or danger daunt, a brick-layer by trade, but one who could turn his hand to anything, the man whom of all others I would choose to have beside me at a pinch; but he's dead. [...]

I said it was time for us to advance again. In fact, it was, perhaps, a little more. By my watch we were three minutes overdue, not altogether a trifle. The artillery were to lift from the next trench at the hour fixed for us to go forward. Our delay meant that the Germans had a chance of reoccupying it, supposing them to have gone to earth under the bombardment. Anyway, when we'd topped a little fold in the ground, we walked straight into a zone of machine-gun fire. The whole line dropped like one man, some dead and wounded, the rest taking instinctively to such cover as the ground offered. On my immediate right three men lay in a shell-hole. With their heads and feet just showing, they looked like fish in a basket.

In crossing no-man's-land we must have lost many more men than I realised then. For the moment the sight of the Germans drove everything else out of my head. Most men, I suppose, have a paleolithic savage somewhere in them, a beast that occasionally shouts to be given a chance of showing his joyful cunning in destruction. I have, anyway, and from the age of catapults to that of shot-guns always enjoyed aiming at anything that moved, though since manhood the pleasure has been sneaking and shamefaced. Now it was a duty to shoot, and there was an easy target. For the Germans were brave men, as brave as lions. Some of them actually knelt – one for a moment even stood – on the top of their parapet, to shoot, within not much more than a hundred yards of us. It was insane. It seemed one couldn't miss them. Every man I fired at dropped, except one. Him, the boldest of the lot, I missed more than once. I was puzzled and angry. Three hundred years ago I should have tried a silver bullet. Not that I wanted to hurt him or anyone else. It was missing I hated. That's the beastliest thing in war, the damnable frivolity. One's like a merry, mischievous ape tearing up the image of God. When I read now the babble of journalists about 'the sporting spirit of our soldiers,' it makes me almost sick. God forgive us all! But then it was as I say. [...]

We attacked, I think, about 820 strong. I've no official figures of casualties. A friend, an officer in 'C' Company, which was in support and shelled to pieces before it could start, told me in hospital that we lost 450 men that day, and that, after being put in again a day or two later, we had 54 left. I suppose it's worth it.

In Parenthesis: David Jones

Mind the hole sir – mind the hole, keep left – go slower in front – they've halted sir.

He pushed forward to investigate.

Is that you sir, Sergeant Snell sir, we've lost connection with No. 6, sir – they must have turned off sir – back there sir.

Where's the guide.

With No. 6 sir.

Lovely for them – we'd better keep the road, get to the rear, see no one falls out, see them all up – move on No. 7, don't lose connection – wait for the man behind – move on.

There's no kind light to lead: you go like a motherless child – goddam guide's done the dirty, and is our Piers Dorian Isambard Jenkins – adequately informed – and

how should his inexperience not be a broken reed for us – and fetch up in Jerry's bosom.
   Slower in front – slower,
not so regardless of this perturbation in the rear; for each false footfall piles up its handicap proportionately backward, and No. 1's mole hill is mountainous for No. 4; and do we trapse dementedly round phantom mulberry bush... can the young bastard know his bearings.

Keep well to left – take care with these messages.
   About their feet the invisible road surface split away in a great, exactly drawn circle; they felt its vacuous pitness in their legs, and held more closely to the banked-up solid.

The rain stopped.
She drives swift and immaculate out over, free of these obscuring waters; frets their fringes splendid.
A silver hurrying to silver this waste
silver for bolt-shoulders
silver for butt-heel-irons
silver beams search the interstices, play for breech-blocks underneath the counterfeiting bower-sway; make-believe a silver scar with drenched tree-wound; silver-trace a festooned slack; faery-bright a filigree with gooseberries and picket-irons – grace this mauled earth –
transfigure our infirmity –
shine on us.
I want you to play with
and the stars as well.
   Received,
curtained where her cloud captors
pursue her bright

pursue her darkly
detain her –
when men mourn for her, who go stumbling [...]

* * *

The repeated passing back of aidful messages assumes a
cadency.
Mind the hole
mind the hole
mind the hole to left
hole right
step over
keep left, left.
   One grovelling, precipitated, with his gear tangled, struggles to feet again:
Left be buggered.
   Sorry mate – you all right china? – lift us yer rifle – an' don't take on so Honey – but rather, mind
the wire here
mind the wire
mind the wire
mind the wire.
   Extricate with some care that taut strand – it may well be you'll sweat on its unbrokenness.

Modulated interlude, violently discorded – mighty, fanned-up glare, to breach it: light orange flame-tongues in the long jagged water-mirrors where their feet go, the feet that come shod, relief bringing – bringing release to these from Wigmore and Woofferton. Weary feet: feet bright, and gospelled, for these, of Elfael and Ceri.

* * *

Sometimes his bobbing shape showed clearly; stiff 75
marionette jerking on the uneven path; at rare intervals
he saw the whole platoon, with Mr Jenkins leading.
   Wired dolls sideway inclining, up and down nodding,
fantastic troll-steppers in and out the uncertain cool
radiance, amazed crook-back miming, where sudden 80
chemical flare, low-flashed between the crazy flats, flood-
lit their sack-bodies, hung with rigid properties –
the drop falls,
you can only hear their stumbling off, across the dark
proscenium. 85

Under Fire: Henri Barbusse

My eyes are getting used to the half-light stagnating in
the cellar and I can more or less make out this line of
people whose dressings and bandages make pale shapes
on their heads and limbs.
   Lame, scarred and deformed, motionless or agitated, 5
clinging to this kind of boat, they seem stuck here, like
the emblems of a varied collection of sufferings and
miseries.
   Suddenly one of them shouts out, half gets up, then
sits down again. His neighbour, bare-headed, wearing a 10
torn overcoat, looks at him and says:
   'Why worry?'
   And he repeats the phrase several times, randomly, his
eyes staring ahead and his hands on his knees.
   A young man sitting in the middle of the bench is 15
talking to himself. He says he's an aviator. He has burns
down one side of his body and on his face. In his fever
he is still burning and believes that he is being licked by

the sharp flames pouring out of the engine. He mutters: '*Gott mit uns!*' and then: 'God is with us!'

A Zouave with his arm in a sling, leaning to one side, carries his shoulder like a terrible burden; he turns to the other man:

'You're the aviator who came down, aren't you?'

'I saw some things,' the aviator replies, painfully.

'Me too,' the soldier interrupts him. 'I've seen some too. There are people who'd go crazy if they saw what I've seen.'

'Come and sit down,' one of the men on the bench says to me, making a place. 'Wounded?'

'No, I brought a wounded man here. I'm going back.'

'Worse than wounded then. Come and sit down.' [...]

'I've got gangrene, I'm crushed, I'm all in pieces inside,' chants one wounded man who has his head in his hands and is talking through his fingers. 'And yet a week ago I was young and clean. They've changed me: now I have only this filthy old body to drag around.'

'I was twenty-six yesterday,' says another. 'How old am I today?'

He tries to get up so that we can see his rickety withered face, worn out in a single night, emptied of flesh, with its sunken cheeks and sockets, and a flame like a night light fading in his oily eye.

'It hurts!' says some invisible creature, humbly.

'Why worry?' says the other man again, mechanically.

There was silence. Then the aviator cried: 'The priests were trying on both sides to disguise their voices!'

'What's that?' said the Zouave in astonishment.

'Are you taking leave of your senses, old chap?' asked a *chasseur* with a wound on the hand, one arm tied to his body, turning away from his mummified hand for a moment to look at the aviator.

He was staring into space, trying to explain the mysterious picture he had in front of his eyes.

'From up there in the sky you don't see much, you know. Among the squares of the fields and the little heaps of villages, roads are like white thread. You can also see some hollow filaments which look as though they were traced with the point of a pin scratched into fine sand. These traces festooning the plain with regular wavy lines are the trenches. On Sunday morning I was flying over the front. Between the edges, between the outer fringe of the two vast armies that are there, one against the other, looking and not seeing one another as they wait, there is very little distance: forty metres in some places, sixty in others. It seemed to me that it was only a step because of the great height at which I was flying. And I could make out two similar gatherings among the Boche and ourselves, in these parallel lines that seem to touch one another: a crowd, a hub of movement and, around it, what looked like black grains of sand scattered on grey ones. They weren't moving; it didn't seem like an alarm! I circled down a bit to get a closer look.

'Then I understood. It was Sunday and these were two services being held in front of my eyes: the altars, the priests and the congregations. The nearer I got the more I could see that these two gatherings were similar – so exactly similar that it seemed ridiculous. One of the ceremonies – whichever you liked – was a reflection of the other. I felt as though I was seeing double.

'I went down further. No one fired at me. Why not? I don't know. Then I heard it. I heard a murmur – a single one. I could only make out one prayer rising up in a single sound, a single hymn rising to heaven and passing through me. I went backwards and forwards in space listening to this vague mixture of songs, one opposing the other, but mingling despite that – and the more they tried to surmount one another the more they were unified in the heights of the sky where I was suspended.

'I was fired at just as, flying very low, I made out the two terrestrial cries of which their one cry was made up: "*Gott mit uns!*" and "God is with us!" – and I flew off.'

The young man shook his head, which was swathed in bandages. It was as though the memory were driving him insane.

'I thought at that moment: "I'm mad!"'

'It's the reality of things that is mad,' said the Zouave.

His eyes blazing with folly, the storyteller tried to convey the great emotion that he felt and against which he was struggling.

'No! Come on!' he exclaimed. 'Imagine those two identical crowds shouting identical yet contrary things: hostile cries that have the same form. What must the good Lord be saying, after all? I realize that he knows everything but even if he does, he can't know what to do.'

'What rubbish!' said the Zouave.

'He doesn't give a damn about us, don't worry.'

'And after all, there's nothing odd about it. Guns speak the same language, don't they, but that doesn't stop countries arguing with them, and how!'

'Yes,' said the aviator. 'But there's only one God. It's not where the prayers come from that bothers me, it's where they go to.'

Letter to Susan Owen: Wilfred Owen

Friday, 19 January 1917   *[2nd Manchester Regiment, British Expeditionary Force]*

We are now a long way back in a ruined village, all huddled together in a farm. We all sleep in the same room where we eat and try to live. My bed is a hammock of rabbit-wire stuck up beside a great shell hole in the wall. Snow is deep about, and melts through the gaping roof, on to my blanket. We are wretched beyond my previous imagination – but safe.

Last night indeed I had to 'go up' with a party. We got lost in the snow. I went on ahead to scout – foolishly alone – and when half a mile away from the party, got overtaken by
      GAS

It was only tear-gas from a shell, and I got safely back (to the party) in my helmet, with nothing worse than a severe fright! And a few tears, some natural, some unnatural.

Here is an Addition to my List of Wants:

Safety Razor (in my drawer) & Blades
Socks (2 pairs)
6 handkerchiefs
Celluloid Soap Box (Boots)
Cigarette Holder (Bone, 3d. or 6d.)
Paraffin for Hair.

(I can't wash hair and have taken to washing my face with snow.)

Coal, water, candles, accommodation, everything is scarce. We have not always air! When I took my helmet off last night – O Air it was a heavenly thing!

Please thank Uncle for his letter, and send the Compass. I scattered abroad some 50 Field Post Cards from the

Base, which should bring forth a good harvest of letters. But nothing but a daily one from you will keep me up.

I think Colin might try a weekly letter. And Father?

We have a Gramophone, and so musical does it seem now that I shall never more disparage one. Indeed I can never disparage anything in Blighty again for a long time except certain parvenus living in a street of the same name as you take to go to the Abbey.

They want to call No Man's Land 'England' because we keep supremacy there.

It is like the eternal place of gnashing of teeth; the Slough of Despond could be contained in one of its crater-holes; the fires of Sodom and Gomorrah could not light a candle to it – to find the way to Babylon the Fallen.

It is pock-marked like a body of foulest disease and its odour is the breath of cancer.

I have not seen any dead. I have done worse. In the dank air I have <u>perceived</u> it, and in the darkness, <u>felt</u>. Those 'Somme Pictures' are the laughing stock of the army – like the trenches on exhibition in Kensington.

No Man's Land under snow is like the face of the moon, chaotic, crater-ridden, uninhabitable, awful, the abode of madness.

To call it 'England'!

I would as soon call my House (!) Krupp Villa, or my child Chlorina Phosgena.

Now I have let myself tell you more facts than I should, in the exuberance of having already done <u>'a Bit.'</u> <u>It is done,</u> and we are all going still farther back for a long time. A long time. The people of England needn't hope. They must agitate. But they are not yet agitated even. Let them imagine 50 strong men trembling as with ague for 50 hours!

                Dearer & stronger love than ever. W.E.O.

Under Fire

Outline: Paul Nash

March 7th, 1917
They stopped post a day before we left, and it was impossible to write again till we got back to our old haunts. We are all sad to leave the quiet of that untroubled country, where such pleasant days have been spent. We could not have hit upon a better time for we saw all the change of trees and fields and hills from bleakness to fresh green and warm lovely lights. I must return to these landscapes above the hills. Just before I left I came upon a bank where real French violets grew, you know those dark ones that have such an intoxicating smell. Alas I was with the Company at the time, and though I meant to hunt out the bank after and send some flowers to you I never had time. Flowers bloom everywhere and we have just come up to the trenches for a time and where I sit now in the reserve line the place is just joyous, the dandelions are bright gold over the parapet and nearby a lilac bush is breaking into bloom; in a wood passed through on our way up, a place with an evil name, pitted and pocked with shells the trees torn to shreds, often reeking with poison gas – a most desolate ruinous place two months back, to-day it was a vivid green; the most broken trees even had sprouted somewhere and in the midst, from the depth of the wood's bruised heart poured out the throbbing song of a nightingale. Ridiculous mad incongruity! One can't think which is the more absurd, the War or Nature; the former has become a habit so confirmed, inevitable, it has its grip on the world just as surely as spring or summer. Thus we poor beings are double enthralled. At the mercy of the old elements which we take pains to study, avoid, build and dress for we are now in the power

of something far more pitiless, cruel and malignant, and so we must study further, build ten times as strong, dress cunningly and creep about like rats always overshadowed by this new terror. Of course we shall get used to it just as we are almost accustomed to the damnable climate of England. Already man has assumed an indifference quite extraordinary to shells, fire, mines and other horrors. It's just as well because it is going to be our daily bread for months and months to come. [...]

Here in the back garden of the trenches it is amazingly beautiful – the mud is dried to a pinky colour and upon the parapet, and through sandbags even, the green grass pushes up and waves in the breeze, while clots of bright dandelions, clover, thistles and twenty other plants flourish luxuriantly, brilliant growths of bright green against the pink earth. Nearly all the better trees have come out, and the birds sing all day in spite of shells and shrapnel. I have made three more drawings all of these wonderful ruinous forms which excite me so much here. We are just by a tumbledown village, only heaps of bricks, toast-rackety roofs and halves of houses here and there among the bright trees and what remains of the orchards. [...]

I feel very happy these days, in fact, I believe I am happier in the trenches than anywhere out here. It sounds absurd, but life has greater meaning here and a new zest, and beauty is more poignant. I never feel dull or careless, always alive to the significance of nature who, under these conditions, is full of surprises for me. I can't quite explain my state of mind, not having troubled to analyse my emotions about it. Last night there was a heavy shelling, in fact the line is not the place it was; the Boche is very restive and jumpy, and I am not surprised. The clouds roll up in these parts and their

shadows already fall over us. I have no fear. I know there
are numerous things I want to say to you, but my mind
is wandering to-day – it's raining and the earth and trees
and all green things exude a moist perfume and make the
soul dream wearily. 70

Counter-Attack: Siegfried Sassoon

We'd gained our first objective hours before
While dawn broke like a face with blinking eyes,
Pallid, unshaved and thirsty, blind with smoke.
Things seemed all right at first. We held their line,
With bombers posted, Lewis guns well placed, 5
And clink of shovels deepening the shallow trench.
    The place was rotten with dead; green clumsy legs
    High-booted, sprawled and grovelled along the saps
    And trunks, face downward, in the sucking mud,
    Wallowed like trodden sand-bags loosely filled; 10
    And naked sodden buttocks, mats of hair,
    Bulged, clotted heads slept in the plastering slime.
    And then the rain began, – the jolly old rain!

A yawning soldier knelt against the bank,
Staring across the morning blear with fog; 15
He wondered when the Allemands would get busy;
And then, of course, they started with five-nines
Traversing, sure as fate, and never a dud.
Mute in the clamour of shells he watched them burst
Spouting dark earth and wire with gusts from hell, 20
While posturing giants dissolved in drifts of smoke.
He crouched and flinched, dizzy with galloping fear,
Sick for escape, – loathing the strangled horror
And butchered, frantic gestures of the dead.

An officer came blundering down the trench: 25
'Stand-to and man the fire-step!' On he went...
Gasping and bawling, 'Fire-step... counter-attack!'
    Then the haze lifted. Bombing on the right
    Down the old sap: machine-guns on the left;
    And stumbling figures looming out in front. 30
'O Christ, they're coming at us!' Bullets spat,
And he remembered his rifle... rapid fire...
And started blazing wildly... then a bang
Crumpled and spun him sideways, knocked him out
To grunt and wriggle: none heeded him; he choked 35
And fought the flapping veils of smothering gloom,
Lost in a blurred confusion of yells and groans...
Down, and down, and down, he sank and drowned,
Bleeding to death. The counter-attack had failed.

Dreamers: Siegfried Sassoon

Soldiers are citizens of death's grey land,
    Drawing no dividend from time's to-morrows.
In the great hour of destiny they stand,
    Each with his feuds, and jealousies, and sorrows.
Soldiers are sworn to action; they must win 5
    Some flaming, fatal climax with their lives.
Soldiers are dreamers; when the guns begin
    They think of firelit homes, clean beds and wives.

I see them in foul dug-outs, gnawed by rats,
    And in the ruined trenches, lashed with rain, 10
Dreaming of things they did with balls and bats,
    And mocked by hopeless longing to regain
Bank-holidays, and picture shows, and spats,
    And going to the office in the train.

Exposure: Wilfred Owen

Our brains ache, in the merciless iced east winds that knive us...
Wearied we keep awake because the night is silent...
Low, drooping flares confuse our memory of the salient...
Worried by silence, sentries whisper, curious, nervous,
    But nothing happens. 5

Watching, we hear the mad gusts tugging on the wire,
Like twitching agonies of men among its brambles.
Northward, incessantly, the flickering gunnery rumbles,
Far off, like a dull rumour of some other war.
    What are we doing here? 10

The poignant misery of dawn begins to grow...
We only know war lasts, rain soaks, and clouds sag stormy,
Dawn massing in the east her melancholy army
Attacks once more in ranks on shivering ranks of grey,
    But nothing happens. 15

Sudden successive flights of bullets streak the silence.
Less deathly than the air that shudders black with snow,
With sidelong flowing flakes that flock, pause, and renew;
We watch them wandering up and down the wind's nonchalance,
    But nothing happens. 20

Pale flakes with fingering stealth come feeling for our faces –
We cringe in holes, back on forgotten dreams, and stare, snow-dazed,

Deep into grassier ditches. So we drowse, sun-dozed,
Littered with blossoms trickling where the blackbird
   fusses.
     – Is it that we are dying? 25

Slowly our ghosts drag home: glimpsing the sunk fires,
   glozed
With crusted dark-red jewels; crickets jingle there;
For hours the innocent mice rejoice: the house is theirs;
Shutters and doors, all closed: on us the doors are
   closed, –
     We turn back to our dying. 30

Since we believe not otherwise can kind fires burn;
Nor ever suns smile true on child, or field, or fruit.
For God's invincible spring our love is made afraid;
Therefore, not loath, we lie out here; therefore were born,
     For love of God seems dying. 35

Tonight, this frost will fasten on this mud and us,
Shrivelling many hands, puckering foreheads crisp.
The burying-party, picks and shovels in shaking grasp,
Pause over half-known faces. All their eyes are ice.
     But nothing happens. 40

The Show: Wilfred Owen

We have fallen in the dreams the ever-living
Breathe on the tarnished mirror of the world,
And then smooth out with ivory hands and sigh.

                                          W.B. YEATS

Under Fire

My soul looked down from a vague height, with Death,
As unremembering how I rose or why,
And saw a sad land, weak with sweats of dearth,
Grey, cratered like the moon with hollow woe,
And pitted with great pocks and scabs of plagues.

Across its beard, that horror of harsh wire,
There moved thin caterpillars, slowly uncoiled.
It seemed they pushed themselves to be as plugs
Of ditches, where they writhed and shrivelled, killed.

By them had slimy paths been trailed and scraped
Round myriad warts that might be little hills.

From gloom's last dregs these long-strewn creatures crept,
And vanished out of dawn down hidden holes.

(And smell came up from those foul openings
As out of mouths, or deep wounds deepening.)

On dithering feet upgathered, more and more,
Brown strings, towards strings of grey, with bristling spines,
All migrants from green fields, intent on mire.

Those that were grey, of more abundant spawns,
Ramped on the rest and ate them and were eaten.

I saw their bitten backs curve, loop, and straighten.
I watched those agonies curl, lift, and flatten.

Whereat, in terror what that sight might mean,
I reeled and shivered earthward like a feather.

And Death fell with me, like a deepening moan. 25
And He, picking a manner of worm, which half had hid
Its bruises in the earth, but crawled no further,
Showed me its feet, the feet of many men,
And the fresh-severed head of it, my head.

Casualties of War

Non-Combatants and Others: Rose Macaulay

Ingram walked by Alix. The yellow leaves drifted suddenly on to the wet road. Alix's hands were as cold as fishes; her lame leg was tired. She talked and laughed. Ingram was talking about dogs – some foolish pug he knew.

Alix too talked of pugs, and chows, and goldfish, and guinea-pigs. Ingram said there had been a pug in his platoon; he told tales of its sagacity and intrepidity in the trenches.

'And then – it was a funny thing – he lost his nerve one day absolutely; simply went to pieces and whimpered in my dug-out, and stayed so till we got back into billets again. He wouldn't come in to the trench again next go; he'd had enough. Funny, rather, because it was so sudden, and nothing special to account for it. But it's the way with some men, just the same. I've known chaps as cheery as crickets, wriggling in frozen mud up to the waist, getting frost-bitten, watching shrapnel and whizz-bangs flying round them as calmly as if they were gnats, and seeing their friends slip up all round them... and never turning a hair. And then one day, for no earthly reason, they'll go to pot – break up altogether. Funny things, nerves...'

Alix suddenly perceived that he knew more about them than appeared in his jolly, sunburnt face; he was talking on rapidly, as if he had to, with inward-looking eyes.

Casualties of War

'Of course there are some men out there who never ought to be there at all; not strong enough in body or mind. There was a man in my company; he was quite young; he'd got his commission straight from school; and he simply went to pieces when he'd been in and out of trenches for a few weeks. He was a nervous, sensitive sort of chap, and delicate; he ought never to have come out, I should say. Anyhow he went all to bits and lost his pluck; he simply couldn't stand the noise and the horror and the wounds and the men getting smashed up round him: I believe he saw his best friend cut to pieces by a bit of shell before his eyes. He kept being sick after that; couldn't stop. And... it was awfully sad... he took to exposing himself, taking absurd risks, in order to get laid out; every one noticed it. But he couldn't get hit; people sometimes can't when they go on like that, you know – it's a funny thing – and one night he let off his revolver into his own shoulder. I imagine he thought he wasn't seen, but he was, by several men, poor chap. No one ever knew whether he meant to do for himself, or only to hurt himself and get invalided back; anyhow things went badly and he died of it... I can tell you this, because you won't know who he was, of course...' (But really he was telling it because, like the Ancient Mariner, he had to talk and tell.) He went on quickly, looking vacantly ahead, 'I was there when he fired... Some of us went up to him, and he knew we'd seen... I shan't forget his face when we spoke to him... I can see it now... his eyes...' He looked back into the past at them, then met Alix's, and it was suddenly as if he was looking again at a boy's white, shamed face and great haunted blue eyes and crooked, sensitive mouth and brows... He stopped abruptly and stood still, and said sharply beneath his breath, 'Oh, good Lord!' Horror started to his face; it mounted and grew as he stared; it leaped from his eyes to the shadowed blue ones he looked into. He guessed what he had done, and, because he guessed, Alix guessed too. Suddenly paler, and very cold and sick, she said, 'Oh...' on a long shivering note; and that too was what the boy in the trenches had said, and how he had said it. Perspiration bedewed the young man's brow, though the air hung clammy and cold about them.

'I beg your pardon,' said Ingram, 'but I didn't hear your name. Do you mind...'

'Sandomir,' she whispered, with cold lips. 'It's the same, isn't it?'

He could not now pretend it wasn't.

'I – I'm sickeningly sorry,' he muttered. 'I'm an ass... a brute... telling you the whole story like that... Oh, I do wish I hadn't. If only you'd stopped me. '

Alix pulled her dazed faculties together. She was occupied in trying not to be sick. It was unfortunate: strong emotion often took her like that; in that too she was like Paul.

'I d-didn't know,' she stammered. 'I never knew before how Paul died. They never said... just said shot...'

He could have bitten his tongue out now.

'You mustn't believe it, please... Sandomir wasn't the name... it was my mistake... Sandberg – that was it.'

'They never said,' Alix repeated. She felt remote from him and his remorse, emptied of pity and drained of all emotions, only very sick, and her hands were as cold as fishes.

Journey's End: R.C. Sherriff

Stanhope stands watching for a moment, then turns and walks slowly to the table. Hibbert comes quietly into the dugout from the tunnel leading from his sleeping quarters.
STANHOPE   Hullo! I thought you were asleep.
HIBBERT   I just wanted a word with you, Stanhope.
STANHOPE   Fire away.
HIBBERT   This neuralgia of mine. I'm awfully sorry. I'm afraid I can't stick it any longer –
STANHOPE   I know. It's rotten, isn't it? I've got it like hell –
HIBBERT   (*taken aback*) *You* have?
STANHOPE   Had it for weeks.
HIBBERT   Well, I'm sorry, Stanhope. It's no good. I've tried damned hard; but I must go down –
STANHOPE   Go down – where?
HIBBERT   Why, go sick – go down the line. I must go into hospital and have some kind of treatment.
There is a silence for a moment. Stanhope is looking at Hibbert – till Hibbert turns away and walks towards his dugout.
   I'll go right along now, I think –
STANHOPE   (*quietly*) You're going to stay here.
HIBBERT   I'm going down to see the doctor. He'll send me to hospital when he understands –
STANHOPE   I've seen the doctor. I saw him this morning. He won't send you to hospital, Hibbert; he'll send you back here. He promised me he would. (*There is silence.*) So you can save yourself a walk.
HIBBERT   (*fiercely*) What the hell – !
STANHOPE   Stop that!

HIBBERT I've a perfect right to go sick if I want to. The men can – why can't an officer?
STANHOPE No man's sent down unless he's very ill. There's nothing wrong with you, Hibbert. The German attack's on Thursday; almost for certain. You're going to stay here and see it through with the rest of us.
HIBBERT (*hysterically*) I tell you, I *can't* – the pain's nearly sending me mad. I'm going; I've got all my stuff packed. I'm going now – *you* can't stop me!
He goes excitedly into the dugout. Stanhope walks slowly towards the steps, turns, and undoes the flap of his revolver holster. He takes out his revolver, and stands casually examining it. Hibbert returns with his pack slung on his back and a walking-stick in his hand. He pauses at the sight of Stanhope by the steps.
HIBBERT Let's get by, Stanhope.
STANHOPE You're going to stay here and do your job.
HIBBERT Haven't I *told* you? I *can't*! Don't you understand? Let – let me get by.
STANHOPE Now look here, Hibbert. I've got a lot of work to do and no time to waste. Once and for all, you're going to stay here and see it through with the rest of us.
HIBBERT I shall die of this pain if I don't go!
STANHOPE Better die of the pain than be shot for deserting.
HIBBERT (*in a low voice*) What do you mean?
STANHOPE You know what I mean –
HIBBERT I've a right to see the doctor!
STANHOPE Good God! Don't you understand! – he'll send you back here. Dr Preston's never let a shirker pass him yet – and he's not going to start now – two days before the attack –

The New Book of Martyrs: Georges Duhamel

Small splinters from a grenade make very little wounds in a man's legs; but great disorders may enter by way of those little wounds, and the knee is such a complicated, delicate marvel!

Corporal Leglise is in bed now. He breathes with difficulty, and catches his breath now and again like a person who has been sobbing. He looks about him languidly, and hardly seems to have made up his mind to live. He contemplates the bottle of serum, the tubes, the needles, all the apparatus set in motion to revive his fluttering heart, and he seems bowed down by grief. He wants something to drink, but he must not have anything yet; he wants to sleep, but we have to deny sleep to those who need it most; he wants to die perhaps, and we will not let him.

He sees again the listening post where he spent the night, in advance of all his comrades. He sees again the narrow doorway bordered by sandbags through which he came out at dawn to breathe the cold air and look at the sky from the bottom of the communication-trench. All was quiet, and the early summer morning was sweet even in the depths of the trench. But some one was watching and listening for the faint sound of his footsteps. An invisible hand hurled a bomb. He rushed back to the door; but his pack was on his back, and he was caught in the aperture like a rat in a trap. The air was rent by the detonation, and his legs were rent, like the pure air, like the summer morning, like the lovely silence. [...]

Casualties of War

[Leglise has one leg amputated. Then the doctors find they need to amputate the other to save his life.]

All humanity at this hour is bearing a very cruel burden. Every minute aggravates its sufferings, and will no one, no one come to its aid?

We made an examination of the wounded man, together with our chief, who muttered almost inaudibly between his teeth:

'He must be prepared for another sacrifice.'

Yes, the sacrifice is not yet entirely consummated.

But Leglise understood. He no longer weeps. He has the weary and somewhat bewildered look of the man who is rowing against the storm. I steal a look at him, and he says at once in a clear, calm, resolute voice:

'I would much rather die.'

I go into the garden. It is a brilliant morning, but I can see nothing, I want to see nothing. I repeat as I walk to and fro:

'He would much rather die.'

And I ask despairingly whether he is not right perhaps.

All the poplars rustle softly. With one voice, the voice of Summer itself, they say: 'No! No! He is not right!'

A little beetle crosses the path before me. I step on it unintentionally, but it flies away in desperate haste. It too has answered in its own way: 'No, really, your friend is not right.'

'Tell him he is wrong,' sing the swarm of insects that buzz about the lime-tree.

And even a loud roar from the guns that travels across the landscape seems to say gruffly: 'He is wrong! He is wrong!'

During the evening the chief came back to see Leglise,

who said to him with the same mournful gravity:

'No, I won't, Monsieur, I would rather die.'

We go down into the garden, and the chief says a strange thing to me:

'Try to convince him. I begin at last to feel ashamed of demanding such a sacrifice from him.'

And I too... am I not ashamed?

I consult the warm, star-decked night; I am quite sure now that he is wrong, but I don't know how to tell him so. What can I offer him in exchange for the thing I am about to ask him? Where shall I find the words that induce a man to live? Oh you, all things around me, tell me, repeat to me that it is sweet to live, even with a body so grievously mutilated.

This morning I extracted a little projectile from one of his wounds. He secretly concluded that this would perhaps make the great operation unnecessary, and it hurt me to see his joy. I could not leave him this satisfaction.

The struggle began again; this time it was desperate. For we have no time to lose. Every hour of delay exhausts our man further. A few days more, and there will be no choice open to him: only death, after a long ordeal...

He repeats:

'I am not afraid, but I would rather die.'

Then I talk to him as if I were the advocate of Life. Who gave me this right? Who gave me eloquence? The things I said were just the right things, and they came so readily that now and then I was afraid of holding out so sure a promise of a life I am not certain I can preserve, of guaranteeing a future that is not in man's hands.

Gradually, I feel his resistance weakening. There is something in Leglise which involuntarily sides with me

Casualties of War

and pleads with me. There are moments when he does 95
not know what to say, and formulates trivial objections,
just because there are others so much weightier.

'I live with my mother,' he says. 'I am twenty years
old. What work is there for a cripple? Ought I to live to
suffer poverty and misery?' 100

'Leglise, all France owes you too much, she would
blush not to pay her debt.'

And I promise again, in the name of our country, sure
that she will never fall short of what I undertake for her.
The whole French nation is behind me at this moment, 105
silently ratifying my promise.

We are at the edge of the terrace; evening has come. I
hold his burning wrist in which the feeble pulse beats
with exhausted fury. The night is so beautiful, so
beautiful! Rockets rise above the hills, and fall slowly 110
bathing the horizon in silvery rays. The lightning of the
guns flashes furtively, like a winking eye. In spite of all
this, in spite of war, the night is like waters dark and
divine. Leglise breathes it in to his wasted breast in long
draughts, and says: 115

'Oh, I don't know, I don't know!... Wait another day,
please, please...'

Disabled: Wilfred Owen

He sat in a wheeled chair, waiting for dark,
And shivered in his ghastly suit of grey,
Legless, sewn short at elbow. Through the park
Voices of boys rang saddening like a hymn,
Voices of play and pleasure after day, 5
Till gathering sleep had mothered them from him.

* * *

About this time Town used to swing so gay
When glow-lamps budded in the light blue trees,
And girls glanced lovelier as the air grew dim, –
In the old times, before he threw away his knees.   10
Now he will never feel again how slim
Girls' waists are, or how warm their subtle hands.
All of them touch him like some queer disease.

* * *

There was an artist silly for his face,
For it was younger than his youth, last year.   15
Now, he is old; his back will never brace;
He's lost his colour very far from here,
Poured it down shell-holes till the veins ran dry,
And half his lifetime lapsed in the hot race
And leap of purple spurted from his thigh.   20

* * *

One time he liked a blood-smear down his leg,
After the matches, carried shoulder-high.
It was after football, when he'd drunk a peg,
He thought he'd better join. – He wonders why.
Someone had said he'd look a god in kilts,   25
That's why; and maybe, too, to please his Meg,
Aye, that was it, to please the giddy jilts
He asked to join. He didn't have to beg;
Smiling they wrote his lie: aged nineteen years.

Germans he scarcely thought of; all their guilt, 30
And Austria's, did not move him. And no fears
Of Fear came yet. He thought of jewelled hilts
For daggers in plaid socks; of smart salutes;
And care of arms; and leave; and pay arrears;
Esprit de corps; and hints for young recruits. 35
And soon, he was drafted out with drums and cheers.

* * *

Some cheered him home, but not as crowds cheer Goal.
Only a solemn man who brought him fruits
Thanked him; and then enquired about his soul.

* * *

Now, he will spend a few sick years in institutes, 40
And do what things the rules consider wise,
And take whatever pity they may dole.
Tonight he noticed how the women's eyes
Passed from him to the strong men that were whole.
How cold and late it is! Why don't they come 45
And put him into bed? Why don't they come?

Non-Combatants

My Heart's Right There: Florence L. Barclay

'Lor', cried Jim, slapping his thigh with his right hand, 'wouldn't it wake up the congregations in some o' these village churches if a shell arrived amongst 'em – slap bang, in the middle of the sermon! Shall I tell you what it's like, Polly, when you lie waiting for them, in the trenches, and they come?

'Well, you can't hear the big guns go off; they're too far away; but you hear the shells coming, for about ten seconds before they burst. It first sounds like wind in the trees. Then it gets louder and louder, gradually going up the scale, till at last it sounds like an express train rushing through a station. Then a hellish row, and the whole ground shakes; then a lot of falling earth comes down; and then, last of all, come what we call "the bees" – pieces of shell that are blown straight up in the air. We call them the bees, because they make a noise like a bee as they come down. That's a lyddite shell; and it's no manner of use being in a funkhole for them; because they dig holes, ten feet broad and six feet deep, on a hard road. The nerve-breaking work is just sitting, waiting for the next shell to come. It's not that one's a bit afraid to die; it's the uncertainty as to whether the *next* shell is going to kill you, or the one after that. A shrapnel shell bursts in the air, and blows out about two hundred lead bullets, just like marbles; and so long as you're in your funkhole for those, it's all right.'

Jim paused. He had been speaking with eager interest, not noticing Polly's whitening face. She tried to hide from him the terror at her heart. She wanted to hear all he could tell; she wanted to know. She forced her voice into a semblance of cheerful unconcern.

'Will it soon be over, Jim?'

'Over?' said Jim. 'Not yet awhile, Polly, this is an *awful* war. In the whole history of the world, there's never been a war like it; and I'll tell you why.

'We ain't only fighting against *men*, out there. We're fighting the Devil... No, my girl. I'm not speaking lightly, nor taking anybody's name in vain. I'm telling you a solemn, awful truth. Wiser an' better men than me, think the same thing. You ask the Archbishop of Canterbury!

'The Boer War was a different thing altogether. I was quite a youngster then, and didn't know much about the rights of it; but we all knew we were fighting *men* – honest men, most of 'em; brave men all of 'em; good old farmers who were fighting, as they thought, for their own homesteads – not wrecking and burning the homes of other people. You see they'd been led into it by one gamey old chap, who thought he could put his big foot down on the British flag, and stand on it. We had to make him step off; we had to hoist the flag, and keep it flying; we had to prove that the Queen was on the throne, and that England knew how to look after her Colonists. But, when it was all over, we could shake hands and be friends. There was respect for each other, and good faith on both sides; and "let's bear no malice."

'But this war, Polly, is more than a fight for earthly crowns and kingdoms; ay, more even than a struggle to keep our homes safe, and our wives and little children free from perils worse than shot and shell. We're fighting for right and justice, against treachery and wrong.

'It's a righteous war, my girl; and every man who fears God and honours the King, should be up, and out, and ready to do his share; and every woman who loves her home, must be willing bravely to do her part, by letting her man go. And if she has to hear that he has given his life, she must stand up, brave and true – as a soldier's wife or a soldier's mother – and say: "God save the King!"'

Jim paused. Polly knew something more was coming. She laid down the khaki Testament, folded her hands and looked up at her husband with lips which trembled, but with a light of earnest resolve in her eyes.

'Polly, my dear girl,' said Jim, slowly; 'when I prayed that, even if I were wounded, I might come home "perfect and entire, wanting nothing," it wasn't to *stay* at home. It was so that I might be fit and able as soon as could be, to go out again. If I had lost an arm or a leg, I should have been done for, where fighting is concerned; but, thank God, I haven't. These wounds will soon heal; you must get me fit as quick as may be; and then I'm off to the Front again; and you must be glad to let me go.'

Polly stood up and faced her big soldier, bravely. Her face was very white and her lips trembled. But the high courage in her eyes matched his.

'God save the King!' said Polly simply.

Non-Combatant: Cicely Hamilton

Before one drop of angry blood was shed
    I was sore hurt and beaten to my knee;
Before one fighting man reeled back and died
    The War-Lords struck at me.

They struck me down – an idle, useless mouth,
    As cumbrous – nay, more cumbrous – than the dead,
With life and heart afire to give and give
    I take a dole instead.

With life and heart afire to give and give
    I take and eat the bread of charity.
In all the length of all this eager land,
    No man has need of me.

That is my hurt – my burning, beating wound;
    That is the spear-thrust driven through my pride!
With aimless hands, and mouth that must be fed,
    I wait and stand aside.

Let me endure it, then, with stiffened lip:
    I, even I, have suffered in the strife!
Let me endure it then – I give my pride
    Where others give a life.

A Journal of Impressions in Belgium: May Sinclair

There is a Taube hovering over Ghent.

Up there, in the clear blue sky it looks innocent, like an enormous greyish blond dragon-fly hovering over a pond. You stare at it, fascinated, as you stare at a hawk that hangs in mid-air, steadied by the vibration of its wings, watching its prey.

You are not in the least disturbed by the watching Taube. An aeroplane, dropping a few bombs, is nothing to what goes on down there where the ambulances are.

The ambulances have come back. I go out into the yard to look at them. They are not always nice to look at; the floors and steps would make you shudder if you were not past shuddering.

I have found something to do. Not much, but still something. I am to look after the linen for the ambulances, to take away the blood-stained pillow-slips and blankets, and deliver them at the laundry and get clean ones from the linen-room. It's odd, but I'm almost foolishly elated at being allowed to do this. We are still more or less weighed down by the sense of our uselessness. Even the Chaplain, though his services as a stretcher-bearer have been definitely recognized – even the Chaplain continues to suffer in this way. He has just come to me to tell me with pride that he is making a good job of the stretchers he has got to mend.

Then, just as I am beginning to lift up my head, the blow falls. Not one member of the Field Ambulance Corps is to be allowed to work at the Palais des Fêtes, for fear of bringing fever into the Military Hospital. And here we are, exactly where we were at the beginning of the week, Mrs Lambert, Janet McNeil and I, three women out of five, with nothing to do and two convalescent orderlies waiting on us. If I could please myself I would tuck Max up in bed and wait on *him*.

In spite of the ambulance linen, this is the worst day of all for the wretched Secretary and Reporter. Five days in Ghent and not a thing done; not a line written of those brilliant articles (from the Front) which were to bring in money for the Corps. To have nothing to do but hang about the Hospital on the off-chance of the Commandant coming back unexpectedly and wanting a letter written; to pass the man with the bullet wound in his mouth a dozen times a day (he is getting very slowly better; his poor face was a little more human this morning); to see the maimed and crippled men trailing and hobbling about the hall, and the wounded carried in on their stretchers – dripping stretchers, agonized bodies, limbs rolled in bandages, blood oozing through the bandages, heads bound with bandages, bandages glued tight to the bone with blood – to see all this and be utterly powerless to help; to endure, day after day, the blank, blond horror of the empty mess-room; to sit before a marble-topped table with a bad pen, never enough paper and hardly any ink, and nothing at all to write about, while all the time the names of places, places you have not seen and never will see – Termonde, Alost, Quatrecht and Courtrai – go on sounding in your brain with a maddening, luring reiteration; to sit in a hateful inactivity, and a disgusting, an intolerable safety, [...] to be profoundly and irrevocably angry with the guileless Commandant, whom at the moment you regard (it may be perversely) as the prime agent in this fatuous sacrifice of women's

Non-Combatants

lives; to want to stop it and to be unable to stop it, and at the same time to feel a brute because you want to stop it – when *they* are enjoying the adventure – I can only say of the experience that I hope there is no depth of futility deeper than this to come. You might as well be taken prisoner by the Germans – better, since that would, at least, give you something to write about afterwards.

What's more, I'm bored.

When I told the Commandant all this he looked very straight at me and said, 'Then you'd better come with us to Termonde.' So straight he looked that the suggestion struck me less as a *bona fide* offer than an ironic reference to my five weeks' funk.

I don't tell him that that is precisely what I want to do. That his wretched Reporter nourishes an insane ambition – not to become a Special Correspondent; not to career under massive headlines in the columns of the *Daily Mail*; not to steal a march on other War Correspondents and secure the one glorious 'scoop' of the campaign. Not any of these sickly and insignificant things. But – in defiance of Tom, the chauffeur – to go out with the Field Ambulance as an *ambulancière*, and hunt for wounded men, and in the intervals of hunting to observe the orbit of a shell and the manner of shrapnel in descending. To be left behind, every day, in an empty mess-room, with a bad pen, utterly deprived of copy or of any substitute for copy, and to have to construct war articles out of your inner consciousness, would be purgatory for a journalist. But to have a mad dream in your soul and a pair of breeches in your hold-all, and to see no possibility of 'sporting' either, is the very refinement of hell. And your tortures will be unbearable if, at the same time, you have to hold your tongue about them and pretend that you are a genuine reporter and that all you want is copy and your utmost aim the business of the 'scoop.'

After a week of it you will not be likely to look with crystal clarity on other people's lapses from precaution.

But it would be absurd to tell him this. Ten to one he wouldn't believe it. He thinks I am funking all the time.

* * *

I am still very angry with him. He must know that I am very angry. I think that somewhere inside him he is rather angry too.

* * *

All the same he has come to me and asked me to give him my soap. He says Max has taken his.

I give him my soap, but –

These oppressions and obsessions, the deadly anxiety, the futile responsibility and the boredom are too much for me. I am thinking seriously of going home.

Mr Britling Sees It Through: H.G. Wells

Mr Britling, after he had looked at his dead cousin for the last time, wandered for an hour or so about the silent little watering-place before he returned to his hotel. There was no one to talk to and nothing else to do but to think of her death.

The night was cold and bleak, but full of stars. He had already mastered the local topography, and he knew now exactly where all the bombs that had been showered upon the place had fallen. Here was the corner of blackened walls and roasted beams where three wounded horses had been burned alive in a barn, here the row of houses, some smashed, some almost intact, where a mutilated child had screamed for two hours before she could be rescued from the débris that had pinned her down, and taken to the hospital. Everywhere by the dim light of the shaded street lamps he could see the black holes and gaps of broken windows; sometimes abundant, sometimes rare and exceptional, among otherwise uninjured dwellings. Many of the victims he had visited in the little cottage hospital where Aunt Wilshire had just died. She was the eleventh dead. Altogether fifty-seven people had been killed or injured in this brilliant German action. They were all civilians, and only twelve were men.

Two Zeppelins had come in from over the sea, and had been fired at by an anti-aircraft gun coming on an automobile from Ipswich. The first intimation the people of the town had had of the raid was the report of this gun. Many had run out to see what was happening. It was doubtful if any one had really seen the Zeppelins, though every one testified to the sound of their engines. Then suddenly the bombs had come streaming down. Only six had made hits upon houses or people; the rest had fallen ruinously and very close together on the local golf links, and at least half had not exploded at all and did not seem to have been released to explode.

A third at least of the injured people had been in bed when destruction came upon them.

The story was like a page from some fantastic romance of Jules Verne's; the peace of the little old town, the people going to bed, the quiet streets, the quiet starry sky, and then for ten minutes an uproar of guns and shells, a clatter of breaking glass, and then a fire here, a fire there, a child's voice pitched high by pain and terror, scared people going to and fro with lanterns, and the sky empty again, the raiders gone...

Five minutes before, Aunt Wilshire had been sitting in the boarding-house drawing-room playing a great stern 'Patience,' the Emperor Patience ('Napoleon, my dear! – not that Potsdam creature') that took hours to do. Five minutes later she was a thing of elemental terror and agony, bleeding wounds and shattered bones, plunging about in the darkness amidst a heap of wreckage. And already the German airmen were buzzing away to sea again, proud of themselves, pleased no doubt – like boys who have thrown a stone through a window, beating their way back to thanks and rewards, to iron crosses and the proud embraces of Fraus and Fräuleins...

For the first time it seemed to Mr Britling he really saw the immediate horror of war, the dense cruel stupidity of the business, plain and close. It was as if he had never perceived anything of the sort before, as if he had been dealing with stories, pictures, shows and representations that he knew to be shams. But that this dear, absurd old creature, this thing of home, this being of familiar humours and familiar irritations, should be torn to pieces, left in torment like a smashed mouse over which an automobile has passed, brought the whole business to a raw and quivering focus. Not a soul among all those who had been rent and torn and tortured in this agony of millions, but was to any one who understood and had been near to it, in some way lovable, in some way laughable, in some way worthy of respect and care. Poor Aunt Wilshire was but the sample thrust in his face of all this mangled multitude, whose green-white lips had sweated in anguish, whose broken bones had thrust raggedly through red dripping flesh…

Armistice

'And There Was a Great Calm': Thomas Hardy

(ON THE SIGNING OF THE ARMISTICE,
Nov. 11, 1918)

I

There had been years of Passion – scorching, cold,
And much Despair, and Anger heaving high,
Care whitely watching, Sorrows manifold,
Among the young, among the weak and old,
And the pensive Spirit of Pity whispered, 'Why?' 5

II

Men had not paused to answer. Foes distraught
Pierced the thinned peoples in a brute-like blindness,
Philosophies that sages long had taught,
And Selflessness, were as an unknown thought,
And 'Hell!' and 'Shell!' were yapped at Lovingkindness. 10

III

The feeble folk at home had grown full-used
To 'dug-outs', 'snipers', 'Huns', from the war-adept
In the mornings heard, and at evetides perused;
To day-dreamt men in millions, when they mused –
To nightmare-men in millions when they slept. 15

IV

Waking to wish existence timeless, null,
Sirius they watched above where armies fell;
He seemed to check his flapping when, in the lull

Armistice

Of night a boom came thencewise, like the dull
Plunge of a stone dropped into some deep well. 20

V

So, when old hopes that earth was bettering slowly
Were dead and damned, there sounded 'War is done!'
One morrow. Said the bereft, and meek, and lowly,
'Will men some day be given to grace? yea, wholly,
And in good sooth, as our dreams used to run?' 25

VI

Breathless they paused. Out there men raised their glance
To where had stood those poplars lank and lopped,
As they had raised it through the four years' dance
Of Death in the now familiar flats of France;
And murmured, 'Strange, this! How? All firing stopped?' 30

VII

Aye; all was hushed. The about-to-fire fired not,
The aimed-at moved away in trance-lipped song.
One checkless regiment slung a clinching shot
And turned. The Spirit of Irony smirked out, 'What?
Spoil peradventures woven of Rage and Wrong?' 35

VIII

Thenceforth no flying fires inflamed the gray,
No hurtlings shook the dewdrop from the thorn,
No moan perplexed the mute bird on the spray;
Worn horses mused: 'We are not whipped to-day';
No weft-winged engines blurred the moon's thin horn. 40

IX

Calm fell. From Heaven distilled a clemency;
There was peace on earth, and silence in the sky;

Some could, some could not, shake off misery:
The Sinister Spirit sneered: 'It had to be!'
And again the Spirit of Pity whispered, 'Why?' 45

Testament of Youth: Vera Brittain

When the sound of victorious guns burst over London at 11 a.m. on November 11th, 1918, the men and women who looked incredulously into each other's faces did not cry jubilantly: 'We've won the War!' They only said: 'The War is over.'

From Millbank I heard the maroons crash with terrifying clearness, and, like a sleeper who is determined to go on dreaming after being told to wake up, I went on automatically washing the dressing bowls in the annex outside my hut. Deeply buried beneath my consciousness there stirred the vague memory of a letter that I had written to Roland in those legendary days when I was still at Oxford, and could spend my Sundays in thinking of him while the organ echoed grandly through New College Chapel. It had been a warm May evening, when all the city was sweet with the scent of wallflowers and lilac, and I had walked back to Micklem Hall after hearing an Occasional Oratorio by Handel, which described the mustering of troops for battle, the lament for the fallen and the triumphant return of the victors.

'As I listened,' I told him, 'to the organ swelling forth into a final triumphant burst in the song of victory, after the solemn and mournful dirge over the dead, I thought with what mockery and irony the jubilant celebrations which will hail the coming of peace will fall upon the ears of those to whom their best will never return, upon whose sorrow victory is built, who have paid with their mourning for the others' joy. I wonder if I shall be one of those who take a happy part in the triumph – or if I shall listen to the merriment with a heart that breaks and ears that try to keep out the mirthful sounds.'

And as I dried the bowls I thought: 'It's come too late for me. Somehow I knew, even at Oxford, that it would. Why couldn't it have ended rationally, as it might have ended, in 1916, instead of all that trumpet-blowing against a negotiated peace, and the ferocious talk of secure civilians about marching to Berlin? It's come five months too late – or is it three years? It might have ended last June, and let Edward, at least, be saved! Only five months – it's such a little time, when Roland died nearly three years ago.'

But on Armistice Day not even a lonely survivor drowning in black waves of memory could be left alone with her thoughts. A moment after the guns had subsided into sudden, palpitating silence, the other V.A.D. from my ward dashed excitedly into the annex.

'Brittain! Brittain! Did you hear the maroons? It's over – it's all over! Do let's come out and see what's happening!'

Mechanically I followed her into the road. As I stood there, stupidly rigid, long after the triumphant explosions from Westminster had turned into a distant crescendo of shouting, I saw a taxicab turn swiftly in from the Embankment towards the hospital. The next moment there was a cry for doctors and nurses from passers-by, for in rounding the corner the taxi had knocked down a small elderly woman who in listening, like myself, to the wild noise of a world released from nightmare, had failed to observe its approach. [...]

Late that evening, when supper was over, a group of elated V.A.D.s who were anxious to walk through Westminster and Whitehall to Buckingham Palace prevailed upon me to join them. Outside the Admiralty a crazy group of convalescent Tommies were collecting specimens of different uniforms and bundling their wearers into flag-strewn taxis; with a shout they seized two of my companions and disappeared into the clamorous crowd, waving flags and shaking rattles. Wherever we went a burst of enthusiastic cheering greeted our Red Cross uniform, and complete strangers adorned with wound stripes rushed up and shook me warmly by the hand. After the long, long blackness, it seemed like a fairly-tale to see the street lamps shining through the chill November gloom.

I detached myself from the others and walked slowly up Whitehall, with my heart sinking in a sudden cold dismay. Already this was a different world from the one that I had known during four life-long years, a world in which people would be light-hearted and forgetful, in which themselves and their careers and their amusements would blot out political ideals and great national issues. And in that brightly lit, alien world I should have no part. All those with whom I had really been intimate were gone; not one remained to share with me the heights and the depths of my memories. As the years went by and youth departed and remembrance grew dim, a deeper and ever deeper darkness would cover the young men who were once my contemporaries.

For the first time I realised, with all that full

realisation meant, how completely everything that had hitherto made up my life had vanished with Edward and Roland, with Victor and Geoffrey. The War was over; a new age was beginning; but the dead were dead and would never return.

Now It Can Be Told: Philip Gibbs

For What Men Died

After the trouble of demobilization came peace pageants and celebrations and flag-wavings. But all was not right with the spirit of the men who came back. Something was wrong. They put on civilian clothes again, looked to their mothers and wives very much like the young men who had gone to business in the peaceful days before the August of '14. But they had not come back the same men. Something had altered in them. They were subject to queer moods, queer tempers, fits of profound depression alternating with a restless desire for pleasure. Many of them were easily moved to passion when they lost control of themselves. Many were bitter in their speech, violent in opinion, frightening. For some time, while they drew their unemployment pensions, they did not make any effort to get work for the future. They said: 'That can wait. I've done my bit. The country can keep me for a while. I helped to save it... Let's go to the "movies."' They were listless when not excited by some 'show.' Something seemed to have snapped in them; their will-power. A quiet day at home did not appeal to them.

'Are you tired of me?' said the young wife, wistfully. 'Aren't you glad to be home?'

Armistice

'It's a dull sort of life,' said some of them.

The boys, unmarried, hung about street-corners, searched for their pals, formed clubs where they smoked incessantly, and talked in an aimless way.

Then began the search for work. Boys without training looked for jobs with wages high enough to give them a margin for amusement, after the cost of living decently had been reckoned on the scale of high prices, mounting higher and higher. Not so easy as they had expected. The girls were clinging to their jobs, would not let go of the pocket-money which they had spent on frocks. Employers favored girl labor, found it efficient and, on the whole, cheap. Young soldiers who had been very skilled with machine-guns, trench-mortars, hand-grenades, found that they were classed with the ranks of unskilled labor in civil life. That was not good enough. They had fought for their country. They had served England. Now they wanted good jobs with short hours and good wages. They meant to get them. And meanwhile prices were rising in the shops. Suits of clothes, boots, food, anything, were at double and treble the price of pre-war days. The profiteers were rampant. They were out to bleed the men who had been fighting. They were defrauding the public with sheer, undisguised robbery, and the government did nothing to check them. England, they thought, was rotten all through.

Who cared for the men who had risked their lives and bore on their bodies the scars of war? The pensions doled out to blinded soldiers would not keep them alive. The consumptives, the gassed, the paralyzed, were forgotten in institutions where they lay hidden from the public eye. Before the war had been over six months 'our heroes,' 'our brave boys in the trenches' were without preference in the struggle for existence.

Later Perspectives on the War

Parade's End: Ford Madox Ford

His eyes met the non-committal glance of a dark, gentlemanly thin fellow with a strikingly scarlet hatband, a lot of gilt about his khaki and little strips of steel chain-armour on his shoulders... Levin... Colonel Levin, G.S.O.II, or something, attached to General Lord Edward Campion... How the hell did fellows get into these intimacies of commanders of units and their men? Swimming in like fishes into the brown air of a tank and there at your elbow – spies!... The men had all been called to attention and stood like gasping codfish. The ever-watchful Sergeant-Major Cowley had drifted to his, Tietjens', elbow. You protect your orfcers from the gawdy Staff as you protect your infant daughters in lambswool from draughts. The dark, bright, cheerful staffwallah said with a slight lisp:

'Busy, I see.' He might have been standing there for a century and have a century of the battalion headquarters' time to waste like that. 'What draft is this?'

Sergeant-Major Cowley, always ready in case his orfcer should not know the name of his unit or his own name, said:

'No. 16 I.B.D. Canadian First Division Casual Number Four Draft, sir.'

Colonel Levin let air lispingly out between his teeth.

'No. 16 Draft not off yet... Dear, dear! Dear, dear!... We shall be strafed to hell by First Army...' He used the word hell as if he had first wrapped it in eau-de-Cologned cotton-wadding.

Tietjens, on his feet, knew this fellow very well: a fellow who had been a very bad Society water-colour painter of good family on the mother's side, hence the cavalry gadgets on his shoulders. Would it then be good... say good taste to explode? He let the sergeant-major do it. Sergeant-Major Cowley was of the type of N.C.O. who carried weight because he knew ten times as much about his job as any Staff officer. The sergeant-major explained that it had been impossible to get off the draft earlier. The colonel said:

'But surely, sergeant-majah...'

The sergeant-major, now a deferential shopwalker in a lady's store, pointed out that they had had urgent instructions not to send up the draft without the four hundred Canadian Railway Service men who were to come from Etaples. These men had only arrived that evening at 5.30... at the railway station. Marching them up had taken three-quarters of an hour. The colonel said:

'But surely, sergeant-majah...'

Old Cowley might as well have said 'madam' as 'sir' to the red hat-band... The four hundred had come with only what they stood up in. The unit had had to wangle everything: boots, blankets, tooth-brushes, braces, rifles, iron-rations, identity discs out of the depot store. And it was now only twenty-one twenty... Cowley permitted his commanding officer at this point to say:

'You must understand that we work in circumstances of extreme difficulty, sir...'

The graceful colonel was lost in an absent contemplation of his perfectly elegant knees.

'I know, of course...' he lisped. 'Very difficult...' He brightened up to add: 'But you must admit you're unfortunate... You must admit that...' The weight settled, however, again on his mind.

Tietjens said:

'Not, I suppose, sir, any more unfortunate than any other unit working under a dual control for supplies...'

The colonel said:

'What's that? Dual... Ah, I see you're there, Mackenzie... Feeling well... feeling fit, eh?'

The whole hut stood silent. His anger at the waste of time made Tietjens say:

'If you understand, sir, we are a unit whose principal purpose is drawing things to equip drafts with...' This fellow was delaying them atrociously. He was brushing his knees with a handkerchief! 'I've had,' Tietjens said, 'a man killed on my hands this afternoon because we have to draw tin-hats for my orderly room from Dublin on an A.F.B. Canadian from Aldershot... Killed here... We've only just mopped up the blood from where you're standing...'

The cavalry colonel exclaimed:

'Oh, good gracious me!...' Jumped a little and examined his beautiful, shining, knee-high aircraft boots. 'Killed!... Here!... But there'll have to be a court of inquiry... You certainly are *most* unfortunate, Captain Tietjens... Always these mysterious... Why wasn't your man in a dug-out?... Most unfortunate... We cannot have casualties among the Colonial troops... Troops from the Dominions, I mean...'

Tietjens said grimly:

'The man was from Pontardulais... not from any Dominion... One of my orderly room... We are forbidden on pain of court martial to let any but

Dominion Expeditionary Force men go into the dugouts... My Canadians were all there... It's an A.C.I. local of the eleventh of November...' 95
  The Staff officer said:
  'It makes, of course, a difference!... Only a Glamorganshire? You say... Oh, well...'

Oh What a Lovely War: Theatre Workshop

CHAPLAIN   Let us pray. O God, show thy face to us as thou didst with thy angel at Mons. The choir will now sing 'What a friend we have in Jesus' as we offer a silent prayer for Sir Douglas Haig for success in tomorrow's onset. 5
SONG: WHEN THIS LOUSY WAR IS OVER
(*Tune:* 'What a friend we have in Jesus')
    When this lousy war is over,
    No more soldiering for me,
    Oh, how happy I shall be!
    No more church parades on Sunday, 10
    No more putting in for leave,
    I shall kiss the sergeant-major,
    How I'll miss him, how he'll grieve!
    Amen.
CHAPLAIN   O Lord, now lettest thou thy servant depart 15
  in peace, according to thy word. Dismiss.
CORPORAL   *(blowing a whistle)* Come on, you men, fall in.
(The soldiers sing as they march off.)
SONG: WASH ME IN THE WATER
    Whiter than the whitewash on the wall,
    Whiter than the whitewash on the wall,

> Oh, wash me in the water that you wash your
> dirty daughter in,
> And I shall be whiter than the whitewash on the
> wall,
> On the wall...

CHAPLAIN Land of our birth we pledge to thee, our love and toil in the years to be.

HAIG Well, God, the prospects for a successful attack are now ideal. I place myself in thy hands.

CHAPLAIN Into thy hands I commend my spirit.

NURSE The fields are full of tents, O Lord, all empty except for as yet unmade and naked iron bedsteads. Every ward has been cleared to make way for the wounded that will be arriving when the big push comes.

HAIG I trust you will understand, Lord, that as a British gentleman I could not subordinate myself to the ambitions of a junior foreign commander as the politicians suggested. It is for the prestige of my King and Empire, Lord.

CHAPLAIN Teach us to rule ourself always, controlled and cleanly night and day.

HAIG I ask thee for victory, Lord, before the Americans arrive.

NURSE The doctors say there will be enormous numbers of dead and wounded, God.

CHAPLAIN That we may bring if need arise, no maimed or worthless sacrifice.

HAIG Thus to grant us fair weather for tomorrow's attack, that we may drive the enemy into the sea.

NURSE O Lord, I beg you, do not let this dreadful war cause all the suffering that we have prepared for. I know you will answer my prayer.

(Explosion. They go off.)

Later Perspectives on the War

MCMXIV: Philip Larkin

Those long uneven lines
Standing as patiently
As if they were stretched outside
The Oval or Villa Park,
The crowns of hats, the sun 5
On moustached archaic faces
Grinning as if it were all
An August Bank Holiday lark;

And the shut shops, the bleached
Established names on the sunblinds, 10
The farthings and sovereigns,
And dark-clothed children at play
Called after kings and queens,
The tin advertisements
For cocoa and twist, and the pubs 15
Wide open all day –

And the countryside not caring:
The place names all hazed over
With flowering grasses, and fields
Shadowing Domesday lines 20
Under wheat's restless silence;
The differently-dressed servants
With tiny rooms in huge houses,
The dust behind limousines;

Never such innocence, 25
Never before or since,
As changed itself to past
Without a word – the men
Leaving the gardens tidy,
The thousands of marriages, 30
Lasting a little while longer:
Never such innocence again.

Strange Meeting: Susan Hill

He could not get used to what the C.O. looked like. He sat on the opposite side of the table, with the wide windows, overlooking the orchard, behind him. It was not dark yet but the lamp was already lit. Perhaps it was that, he thought, perhaps Garrett looked better in the 5 undistorting daylight. But it was not that, not just an expression. Everything about him had changed. [...]

Hilliard thought, I have been away five weeks and he is twenty years older, he is... He could not take it in.

From the beginning of his time here he had liked 10 Colonel Garrett, had got on well with him, though without holding him in the same sort of esteem he had held Ward, the dead Captain of B company. But the C.O. had befriended him, had seen that he was as comfortable as any man could be, that spring on the 15 Somme. He made a point of keeping in touch, of sending for and talking to his subalterns as well as the senior officers, he came down into the trenches frequently.

Garrett had trained as a lawyer before taking his army 20 commission and he still seemed much more like a solicitor than a soldier, though he had been in the army for so long. Hilliard wondered why he *was* in the army. He knew that Garrett had a wife and four daughters somewhere, in Worthing or Horsham or Lewes. He was not an imaginative man. But careful, a good planner, cool headed. Perhaps all that simply meant, brave.

Within the space of five weeks, and those after two years of consistent service in the Old Front Line, his air of calm and the slight ponderousness had vanished. His face was altered, was thinner, the eyes puffed but the cheeks drawn in, his fingers moved all the time about the rim of his glass, or smoothed down the patch of thinning hair. Mons, Le Cateau and Ypres, and then the first battle of the spring offensive had not shaken him. So what had the past month been like? Hilliard was appalled, he had not dreamed that this could happen and so quickly to a man like Garrett. To a man who was yet not ill or wounded, who had survived for so long by careful management, perhaps, and luck. Well, and he still survived, he was here. An old man in the yellow-grey lamplight.

It was possible to see what this room of the farmhouse had been like as a parlour: there was a wide stone fireplace and an uneven floor, you could imagine old soft sofas and coarse mats, stone jugs full of marigolds and cornflowers. The windows, long and loose in their frames, shaken by past shelling, were open now. The smells of the autumn evening came in, of grass and trees and rotting fruit, and the army smells, tobacco and bullet smoke, horses and cooking.

The guns were booming like summer thunder, away in the distance.

'You lost Bates, of course.'

'Yes.'

Later Perspectives on the War

'I think Coulter's a good man, isn't he? You'll be all right with Coulter.'

'Yes.'

For a moment, he wondered whether nothing else might be said, whether Garrett would not want, after all, to go over what had happened, preferring to leave the summer behind him. There were too many names to bring up, too many individual deaths.

Silence. The C.O. jerked his head and looked behind him suddenly, as though he had heard something unusual, and then turned back again. Hilliard could not get over his face, the change in his face. He waited for the usual questions about home.

'We lost three quarters of the Battalion in a day and a half. Getting on for two dozen officers. Major Gadney, young Parkinson, Ward – all the best. Half of them went because we didn't receive an order telling us the second push was cancelled. They just went on. You were well out of it. I'm glad you were out of it.'

Hilliard did not speak.

'I've seen nothing like it. Nothing. Not that we were the only ones. They went mad, we might have been a pack of schoolboys in a scrum. Did you hear about the Jocks? Most of them went straight on to the wire. They were on our right, we watched it. The sun was shining, you could see for miles, even through the smoke, we just watched them go. We lost Pearcy and thirty-eight men all in one go. I'd just gone down there, I saw them. God alone knows what was supposed to be going on. I didn't. I haven't found out yet. None of us knows. I suppose it's all on paper somewhere. Nothing came through to us at all, everything went to blazes, telephones, runners. Half the artillery blew themselves up with their own Lewis guns backfiring because somebody hadn't attended to them properly. Most of Parkinson's lot went up with a mine. There was a barrage they didn't tell us about and we couldn't get word through to them to stop, we were running into our own covering fire. And then they started to shoot machine guns from the left flank, they'd lost their bearings, they thought we were Boche. Not surprising. After an hour or so you couldn't see a thing. It was a day and a half, two days, of absolute bloody chaos. Bloody pointless mess.'

Hilliard realized that this was what had upset his careful lawyer's mind more than anything else, this lack of order and reason. The mess.

'And then we had another full week without any relief, and most of our support line gone.'

All the time he spoke he turned the whisky glass round and round in his hand, so that the lamplight caught it. Hilliard could not piece the story together, could not picture what might have happened in the battle, any more than Garrett could remember. He did not even know exactly when it had been. It did not matter. He had only to listen.

'It was about eighty degrees during the day. I've never known it so hot.'

He remembered the heat, in the ward of the military hospital. They had pulled down the green blinds but it had felt no cooler. The Field-Gunner had tossed about, crying all day as he cried all night.

'You were well out of it.'

'Yes.'

'Clifford went berserk. Do you remember Clifford? Swarthy looking chap, bit of a gypsy. Went completely

berserk, they couldn't hold him down, couldn't shut him up, couldn't do anything with him at all.'
'Was he hurt?'
'No.'
'What happened in the end, then?'
'Oh, he shot himself.'

Garrett's voice trailed off. Hilliard did not remember the man, Clifford, but that did not matter, either. He wondered how long it was since Garrett had talked so freely. Talked at all.

Observe the Sons of Ulster Marching Towards the Somme: Frank McGuinness

A trench, the Somme. McIlwaine, the Younger Pyper and Millen are awake. The others sleep.

MCILWAINE   You'd think they were dead, it's that quiet.
PYPER   Yes.
MILLEN   When do you think word'll come?
PYPER   When we're ready.
MILLEN   What have we to do with it?
PYPER   We do the attacking.
MILLEN   We don't do the ordering.
PYPER   You above all are not beginning to panic Millen?
MILLEN   I've been panicking since the last leave, Pyper.
MCILWAINE   There won't be much of daylight before we're going over.
MILLEN   I think this is it. I think this is going to be the end.
PYPER   Millen, for Christ's sake.
MILLEN   I can't help it. I know this time.

Later Perspectives on the War

MCILWAINE   Nobody knows nothing here.
PYPER   Any officers about?
MCILWAINE   One passed twenty minutes ago. Told us to get some rest.
MILLEN   I saw him. Useless bugger. Surely to God they're not going to trust us with that piece of work. Where do they dig them out of anyway? Superior rank, is that it? Superior, my arse.
MCILWAINE   Keep talking like that and it'll be a court martial you'll be facing, not –
MILLEN   Let me face it and I'll tell them straight.
PYPER   Tell them what?
MILLEN   What they're doing to us.
MCILWAINE   And that will stop them? That'll stop us? Save your breath for running. It's a bit late to start crying now.
MILLEN   I'm not crying.
MCILWAINE   You're damn near it. Pyper? You come from a swanky family, don't you?
PYPER   Why ask that now?
MCILWAINE   I'm just beginning to wonder what you're doing down with us instead of being with them.
PYPER   And who are they?
MCILWAINE   Top brass.
PYPER   I'm not top brass, McIlwaine. Maybe once. Not now. I blotted my copybook.
MCILWAINE   How?
MILLEN   Should we waken the boys?
MCILWAINE   Give them time to dream. How, Pyper?
PYPER   Just being the black sheep.
MCILWAINE   Bit of a wild one?
PYPER   Bit.
MCILWAINE   Like myself. I broke the mother's heart.

PYPER   I broke my mother's arm. More practical, more painful.
MILLEN   Pyper, how can you laugh at a time like this?
PYPER   I'm not laughing, Millen.
MILLEN   Have you contacts up above there? Ones posted to watch over you and make sure you end up in some cushy corner? Is that why you can laugh?
PYPER   Get something into that thick Coleraine skull of yours, Millen. Nobody's watching over me except myself. What the hell has got into you?
MILLEN   What got into you the first time we met you. Remember? Knowing we're all going to die. Knowing we're all going...
(McIlwaine grabs Millen)
MCILWAINE   One minute, you. Just one minute. These chaps are having a well-earned kip. Now they're not going to come to their senses listening to a squealing woman keening after death. Do you hear? If you want to make traitors of them, you'll deal with me first. And if you want out, start marching now.
MILLEN   I've never run away from what I had to do. I commanded –
PYPER   We all know that. But there's more than sixteen-year-old Fenians you're up against now. Will that hit you once and for all?
MCILWAINE   I'm warning you.
PYPER   Let him go, McIlwaine.
MILLEN   I never thought I was a coward.
MCILWAINE   You're not a coward. You've done enough to prove that.
MILLEN   But I'm a soldier.
MCILWAINE   You're a man. The shit's scared out of you. Do you think you're on your own?
MILLEN   No.
MCILWAINE   Well then.

Later Perspectives on the War

Waiting for the Telegram: Alan Bennett

Verity fetches a young lad in this morning. She says to him, 'You're privileged. Violet is our oldest resident.' She says, 'Spencer's going to ask you one or two questions for his school project. It's about the past.'

Poor-looking lad, bonny face. Floppy clothes, shirt-tail out. I said 'Is that your big brother's jumper?' He says, 'No. It's dead smart, is this.' Gets out his exercise book, and says, 'What was it like then?' I said, 'Well...' He said, 'Were things better or worse?' I said, 'Well, my legs were better.' He said he didn't mean that. Verity comes back and he says, 'She doesn't seem to know what I'm talking about.' Verity says, 'Well, she's had a stroke. Come on, I'll find you another one.' (*Violet is a bit upset.*)

I said to Francis, 'He'd mean trams and whatnot. Strikes. Tin-baths. The war.' Francis says, 'Which war?' I said, 'The proper war when all the young lads got killed. "Never again." That war.' He looked right sad and said, 'Hold my hand.' So I did. Then he said, 'Did you have a young man?' I said, 'Yes.' He said, 'What was he like?' I said, 'His name was Edward. They had a little confectioner's down Tong Road. He used to fetch my mam a vanilla slice. Every time he came round, a vanilla slice.'

I still had hold of his hand. I said, 'When you were courting then, it was a kind of... where you fight...' He said, 'Struggle.' I said 'Ay. He'd manage to get one button undone one night, and another the next. And lasses weren't supposed to do much in them days, just lie back and get ready to draw the line. And because I'd let him get so far one night, he'd know where the front line was, so the next night he'd get there a bit quicker and push on a bit further... another button, you know. It

Later Perspectives on the War

was that... grudging somehow. But it was the way you felt you had to be then.

'Anyway he was going off to France next day; he was in camp over at Church Fenton and they'd given him a pass for his last night. My mam... oh she was a good 'un... she put some anemones in a vase... I love anemones... and put a fire in the front room and then she reckoned she had to stay at my Aunt Florence's that night. Ordinary folks then were better than they're ever given credit for, for all they were so straitlaced.

'I gave him his tea and then we went and sat in the front room and he started on like, undoing my buttons and kissing and whatnot. Only I'd wanted to look nice so I'd put on my best frock and he couldn't fathom how it unfastened. I should just have taken it off but I didn't and, poor lamb, he got so fed up with these flaming buttons, in the finish he gave up.

'He'd taken his leggings... his puttees off because they were hot and he was in his shirtsleeves; they were right rough khaki shirts then, really cheap and itchy. Anyway in the finish he gets up off the sofa and says, "Hang this lot," and he takes his shirt off and everything else besides. Doesn't say a word, just takes it all off and stands there on the hearthrug. Oh and he looked a picture, with the fire and that. Not a mark on him. Then he says, "Take your clothes off now."

(She covers her face with her hands.)

'And I didn't. I didn't. And I wanted him so much. I don't know... it was just the way I'd been brought up. And he stands there looking down at me... and then he just picks his clothes up and goes next door and after a bit I heard the front door bang.

'They look old in photographs compared with what

they look now. Only they weren't. They were lads, same as you. And just as grand.

(Pause)

'I saw the yellow thing the boy on the bike brings... his sister fetches it round... telegram. And a vanilla slice for mam. Then later on they had a letter reckoning to be from the King, same as everybody did who'd lost somebody. They keep saying I'll be getting a telegram soon... for my birthday.'

Francis says, 'Do you know something, Violet? In all that, you never said, "What do you call it?" or "What's its name?" Not once. You knew all the words.'

'Only I should have let him, shouldn't I? I've never forgiven myself.'

'Well,' Francis says, 'how can you know?'

Notes

Outbreak of war

The Vigil: Henry Newbolt

Sir Henry Newbolt (1862–1938) was already an established literary figure in the late Victorian era. He was a lawyer, and he wrote plays and novels as well as poetry in a heroic style promoting traditional qualities such as chivalry and sportsmanship. In his most famous poem, *Vitaï Lampada*, a young officer encourages his troops in battle with the same rallying cry as the captain of his school cricket team: 'Play up! play up! and play the game!' Poems like these were enormously popular at the beginning of the First World War. During the war, Newbolt worked in the British War Propaganda Bureau, helping to influence public opinion in favour of the war effort.

The Vigil is considered to be the first poem of the war. It was printed in *The Times* on the morning of 5 August 1914; Britain's ultimatum to Germany had expired the previous evening (see page 104, Note to line 47). Newbolt had in fact written the poem 16 years earlier, but later claimed to have done so with a kind of mystical foreknowledge of what was to come.

7 **Watch beside thine arms to-night** According to the medieval tradition of chivalry, a young squire about to receive his knighthood would spend the night before the ceremony praying alone in church. This was known as the 'Vigil at Arms'. His arms (weapons) would be placed on the altar as a reminder that they were only to be used in the service of God.
13 **ruth** pity, compassion.
20 **Gordon, Outram** Two English generals who were regarded as national heroes for their services to the British Empire in the nineteenth century. General Charles Gordon fought in the Crimean War and campaigns in China and Africa, while

Notes

> General Sir James Outram helped to suppress the Indian rebellion of 1857–8.

Chronicle of Youth (Great War Diary 1913–1917): Vera Brittain

In 1914, Vera Brittain was 20 and had just met Roland Leighton, who was to become her fiancé, when the war interrupted their lives. She had fought long and hard to gain a place at Oxford University, but when Roland, her brother Edward and their friends had all gone to the Front, Brittain left her studies to become a Voluntary Aid Detachment (VAD) nurse and served in army hospitals for the remainder of the war.

A writer, feminist and lifelong peace activist, she is best known for her memoir *Testament of Youth* (1933, see page 82), which explores the impact of the war on the young people of her generation and her own experience of devastating loss: Roland, Edward and their two best friends were all killed in action.

This extract is from a diary she kept during the first half of the war.

- 6 **Armageddon** an epic battle that will mark the end of the world, according to prophesies in the Abrahamic religions (Judaism, Christianity and Islam).
- 31 **Zeppelins** rigid airships, which the German military used as scouts and bombers.
- 47 **ultimatum** On 4 August, Prime Minister Herbert Asquith had asked the German Government for 'a satisfactory assurance as to the Belgian neutrality before midnight tonight'.
- 62–3 **Territorials, Reservists** The Territorial Force consisted of part-time, voluntary soldiers, who had signed up for Home Service; Reservists were those who had already completed a term of service with the regular army.
- 88 **Liège** The first land battle of the war was fought at Liège, when the Germans invaded neutral Belgium in order to reach Paris by the most direct route. The Belgians put up a strong resistance, but were eventually defeated on 15 August.

Notes to pages 15–22

Song of the Soldiers (Men Who March Away): Thomas Hardy

Thomas Hardy is best known for the novels he wrote during the Victorian era, but he was also a great poet; he wrote poetry on a wide range of subjects from the 1860s until his death in 1928. Generally, his attitude to war was negative. He had already written imaginatively and questioningly about the effects of war in poems such as *A Wife in London* and *Drummer Hodge*, written during the Anglo-Boer war of 1899–1902.

However, in August 1914, soon after war was declared, Charles F.G. Masterman, who had been put in charge of what eventually became the Ministry of Information (the War Propaganda Bureau), called together a group of well-known writers for, as Hardy recorded in his journal, 'the organisation of public statements of the strength of the British case and principles in the war'. Hardy apparently went straight home from the meeting and wrote *Men Who March Away*. The poem was printed in *The Times* on 9 September 1914, and then appeared in the volume *Songs and Sonnets for England in Wartime*.

  8 **purblind** nearly or partly blind; lacking insight. The speaker – one of the soldiers – wonders if the unhappy-looking observer thinks the whole thing is a stupid trick.

The Call: R.E. Vernède

Also included in *Songs and Sonnets for England in Wartime* (see above), *The Call* encourages young men to enlist in language that suggests a religious vocation. Robert Vernède, a novelist and poet, became an army officer in 1915, at the age of 40. He was wounded at the Battle of the Somme, and killed in 1917.

  16 From the Bible, John 15:13: 'Greater love hath no man than this, that a man lay down his life for his friends.'
  18 **faerie brew** Various legends tell of herbal potions that bestow magical powers.

Notes

    42 **betide**   happen, come about.
    47 **him who deathless died**   Jesus Christ.

On Receiving News of the War: Isaac Rosenberg

Isaac Rosenberg was staying in Cape Town, South Africa, when he heard that war had broken out. He was an artist and poet, struggling to make a living, and although he was critical of the war from the start, he returned to England in 1915 and joined the army as a private soldier, partly for financial reasons. His later poems from the trenches are considered to be among the finest writing of the war. He was killed in April 1918 at the age of 27.

This poem is very different in style and mood from those in *Songs and Sonnets for England in Wartime* (see above). What attitudes to the war does Rosenberg convey? You may like to compare the last stanza with the ideas in the passage from Edmund Gosse (page 24) and Rupert Brooke's sonnet (page 25).

Conflict begins

War and Literature: Edmund Gosse

Edmund Gosse (1849–1928) was an established literary figure of the Edwardian era. He had lectured in English literature at Cambridge University, was an influential art critic, wrote several volumes of poetry, and in 1914 had just retired from being librarian to the House of Lords. In the essay 'War and Literature', written in autumn 1914, he puts forward the view that life in Edwardian England (for those of his social class, at any rate) had grown too luxurious, decadent and complacent. War would clean things up – it would bring hardship, but also the ideals of dedication and sacrifice.

    2–3 **Condy's Fluid**   a disinfectant solution developed and
         marketed in the 1850s by Henry Condy, a London chemist.
     14 **poltroonery**   cowardice, lack of spirit.

20–21 **'Slaughter is God's daughter'**   This misquotation refers to a phrase not from Coleridge (22), but from William Wordsworth's *Ode XLV* ('Thanksgiving Ode'). These lines, which were much criticized, appeared only in the first version. Wordsworth altered them in later versions:

> But Thy most dreaded instrument
> In working out a pure intent,
> Is man arrayed for mutual slaughter:
> Yea, Carnage is Thy daughter.

Give us Men!: The Bishop of Exeter

This propaganda poem was printed and distributed on postcards, with the first letter of the poem set within a small detail of a cherub.

Archibald Robertson was Bishop of Exeter from 1903 until 1916. He was also known for donating money from the Cathedral Maintenance Fund to the Archbishop and Mayor of Malines, in Belgium, which was badly damaged in the early weeks of the war.

The Dead (Sonnet 3): Rupert Brooke

Rupert Brooke's sequence of five sonnets entitled *1914* was widely read and received with great enthusiasm early in the war. The sonnets, which present a highly idealistic view of young men going to war, have been described as supreme expressions of English patriotism. However, as the war dragged on and disillusionment set in, they fell out of favour. Brooke, who was born in 1887, had a promising literary career and was one of the founders of Georgian poetry. He joined the Royal Naval Volunteer Reserve, but died of blood poisoning at sea in 1915 without taking part in active service.

A Subaltern on the Somme: Max Plowman

The poet Max Plowman (1883–1941) was opposed to the war from the start, but felt obliged to play his part. Having signed up

Notes

to work with the Territorial Field Ambulance at the end of 1914, he served on the Somme during 1916, but was sent home to recover from shell shock. Like Siegfried Sassoon (see page 6), he wanted to make a formal protest against the war. In January 1918, he declared himself a conscientious objector; he was arrested, court-martialled and dismissed from the army. Later, in the 1930s, he was secretary to the Peace Pledge Union. His memoir *A Subaltern on the Somme* was written in the late 1920s.

- 19 **puttees** a wide khaki bandage wound around the legs from the ankle to just below the knee, sealing the gap between boots and trousers.
- 38 ***The Globe*** a British newspaper that was suppressed in November 1915 for failing to conform to government propaganda requirements.
- 49–50 **Love's embodiment** i.e. their child.
- 70 **'all silent and all…'** This is a quotation from a stanza in the original (1819) version of *Peter Bell*, a long poem by Wordsworth, which was omitted in later versions. The character in the poem, out in the dark, hallucinates that a forbidding group of rocks is a supernatural party in hell:

  Is it a party in a parlour?
  Crammed just as they on earth were crammed, –
  Some sipping punch, some sipping tea,
  But, as you by their faces see,
  All silent and all damned.

  Plowman suggests that the men in the railway carriage look like a party of 'damned' ghosts.

The 'enemy'

Christmas 1914: Frederick Chandler

The events of Christmas 1914 have become legendary: an unofficial truce occurred at several locations along the Western

Front. 'Enemies' emerged from the trenches to meet in No Man's Land, small gifts and tokens were exchanged and, according to some witnesses, games of football took place. The generals were furious when they heard of this and strict orders were issued forbidding fraternization with the enemy. From 1915 onwards, artillery bombardments were specially ordered for Christmas Eve, to avoid any repetition of such incidents.

Frederick Chandler was the Medical Officer to the 2nd Argyll and Sutherland Highlanders. The extract is from an article, based on letters to his family, which he wrote a year later. It was printed in the *London Hospital Gazette* in December 1915.

  16   **haus-frau**   (house)wife.
31–2   **bully beef**   tinned corned beef.

To Germany: Charles Hamilton Sorley

Charles Hamilton Sorley's was one of the first questioning voices to become popular when his poems were published posthumously early in 1916. Immediately before the war Sorley had spent six months studying in Germany, where he 'fell in love' with the country and its culture. Although he returned to England and joined up, he was not enthusiastic and often expressed impatience with conventional patriotic attitudes and anti-German propaganda.

Sorley was killed at the Battle of Loos in October 1915 at the age of 20, and although he completed only 37 poems, his work is highly regarded. In his memoir *Goodbye to All That*, Robert Graves describes Sorley as 'one of the three poets of importance killed during the war'.

In this poem, it is clear that he regards neither side as more right or wrong than the other. The war seems to be the tragic and ironic result of mutual ignorance.

Letter to Vera Brittain: Roland Leighton

The relationship of Roland Leighton (1895–1915) with Vera Brittain (see page 104) is immortalized in her *Testament of Youth*

Notes

(see page 82). A promising scholar, he was due to go to Oxford University, but when war broke out, he obtained a commission and went to France. They became engaged while he was home on leave in August 1915 and wrote to each other frequently, discussing literature, politics and their experience of the war. She had asked him to be open with her about the realities of war, although censorship would have limited what he could say.

Six weeks earlier, Brittain had enthusiastically sent Leighton a copy of Rupert Brooke's sonnet collection *1914* (see page 107). His response shows that he was already questioning the idealized view shown in Brooke's sonnets: 'it is only War in the abstract that is beautiful. Modern warfare is merely a trade.'

Here Leighton describes supervising a digging party on the site of former German trenches. He was killed less than four months later, just when Brittain was expecting him home on leave for Christmas.

12–13 **poured out their red, sweet wine of youth unknowing** See Brooke, *The Dead*, page 25. Re-read Brooke's poem and compare the tone of Leighton's comments.
14–15 **Honour, Glory, Lust, Power** Why has Leighton capitalized words such as these?
   19 **priests of Baal** Baal was a god in eastern Mediterranean traditions. According to the Bible (1 Kings 18), the prophet Elijah demonstrates the power of God in a contest with 450 priests of Baal, who offer fervent prayers and sacrifices but receive no response from their god. Leighton makes the point that grand words about war are equally pointless.

A Dead Boche: Robert Graves

Robert Graves (1895–1985) had just left school when the war began. He joined the army and became a captain in the Royal Welsh Fusiliers, but became critical of the way the war was being handled by those in power. He was a friend of Siegfried Sassoon (see page 118), who influenced his work. He wrote about his war experiences in three volumes of poetry as well as his acclaimed autobiography, *Goodbye to All That*.

Boche is a disparaging term commonly used for German soldiers. This unsentimental, graphic portrait of a German victim is designed to shock the reader into questioning the traditional view of war. Graves simply confronts us with a horrific sight. He does not comment, express pity, or mitigate his description in any way. How does the poem impact on you as a reader?

Under fire

France at War: Rudyard Kipling

Rudyard Kipling was already a popular author and poet in the late Victorian era. He was born in India and worked there during the 1880s, and was deeply imbued with the colonial culture and lifestyle. He was a brilliant storyteller and is best known for his collections of tales for young people and adults such as *The Jungle Book* and *Just So Stories*, as well as stirring poetry for and about the soldiers of the British Empire. He received the Nobel Prize for Literature in 1907.

Although he was not in sympathy with the Liberal government at the start of the war, Kipling did become involved in propaganda work, and wrote pamphlets supporting the war effort. In 1915 he travelled to France as a journalist. He visited French troops on the Western Front and wrote a series of articles for the *Daily Telegraph* in England and the *New York Sun*. Later these were collected and published in booklet form.

The extract here is from the first article, which appeared on 6 September 1915, entitled 'On the Frontier of Civilization'.

39–40 **yellow grass**   The officer explains (41) that gas has been used here. This would have been mustard gas, which did turn grass yellow. It was the first form of gas or chemical weapon to be used in the First World War.

Notes

- 40 **the veldt** open country characteristic of southern Africa.
- 52 **groyne** post or barrier on a beach, designed to reduce coastal erosion.
- 53 **seventh wave** It is said – by surfers, for example – that every seventh wave is larger than the others.
- 55 **torpilleurs** small mortars used to clear out trenches before an attack.
- 90–91 **from here to the sea or to Switzerland** The trench system of the Western Front did stretch from the North Sea to Switzerland.
- 99 **frontier of civilization** The influence of propaganda comes across clearly here, as the war is clearly seen in terms of right and wrong, as a battle against the uncivilized, 'barbaric' (see 102) Germans.

The Attack: R.H. Tawney

The well-known historian and social critic R.H. Tawney (1880–1962) served as a sergeant with the 22nd Manchester Regiment in the First World War. He was offered a commission as an officer, but refused on account of his strong socialist beliefs. He was wounded on the first day of the Battle of the Somme and lay in No Man's Land for 30 hours before he was rescued by the medical corps.

This extract is taken from an account of his experience that was published in the *Westminster Gazette* in August 1916. As well as a vivid attempt to capture the sights and sounds of battle, it contains psychologically interesting reflections on his state of mind and his attitude to war.

- 8 **unwonted** unusual, out of the ordinary.
- 24 *butte* small hill.
- 38–9 **The sound was different** Note the variety of language and imagery Tawney uses in the following lines as he tries to convey the sound and impact of the bombardment.
- 78 *The Pilgrim's Progress* a Christian allegory written by John Bunyan in 1677–8, which tells the story of Christian's struggles and 'progress' as he journeys through life from this world (the City of Destruction) to heaven (the Celestial City).

97 **Saint-Just** Louis Antoine de Saint-Just, eighteenth-century French revolutionary and military leader.
113 **at a pinch** in an emergency.
130 **paleolithic** stone age.

In Parenthesis: David Jones

David Jones (1895–1974) enlisted as a private with the Royal Welsh Fusiliers in 1914 and served on the Western Front until the end of the war. His later painting and poetry were deeply influenced by his experiences in the trenches. *In Parenthesis* is an unusual work; it is a long prose-poem in which he explores 'some things I saw, felt & was part of' between December 1915 and July 1916, although it was not published until 1937. It is 'modernist' in style, and T.S. Eliot regarded it as 'a work of genius… a work of literary art which uses the language in a new way'. In it we hear the voices of the men who were Jones's companions in the war – 'mostly Londoners with an admixture of Welshmen'. For example, notice the use of Cockney rhyming slang, and Welsh names and intonation.

Jones wrote his own explanatory notes on the text. They are included here in *italics*.

Title **In Parenthesis** Literally, a word or phrase *in parenthesis* is one that is inserted (often in brackets) into a sentence that would make complete sense without it. The phrase also suggests a digression, an interval or interlude. The title suggests that Jones's war experience felt like a separate existence, bracketed off from the rest of his life.

13 **no kind light to lead** This refers to the words of a well-known hymn written in 1833 by Cardinal John Henry Newman:

> Lead, kindly Light, amid the encircling gloom,
> Lead Thou me on!
> The night is dark, and I am far from home –
> Lead Thou me on!
> Keep Thou my feet; I do not ask to see
> The distant scene – one step enough for me.

Notes

13–14 **like a motherless child** In the words of the traditional negro spiritual, 'Sometimes I feel/ Like a motherless child/ A long way from home.'

16 **broken reed** This is a reference to the Bible, Isaiah 36:6: 'Lo, thou trusteth in the staff of this broken reed, on Egypt; whereon if a man lean, it will go into his hand, and pierce it.' As an inexperienced leader, Jenkins (15) may do more harm than good and lead them into the German lines (*Jerry's bosom*).

22–3 **round phantom mulberry bush** This phrase comes from the nursery rhyme and children's singing game, 'Here we go round the mulberry bush'.

33–5 **bolt-shoulders, butt-heel-irons, breech-blocks** metal parts of the firearms the soldiers are carrying.

38 **festooned slack** *'field-telephone wires, which were a frequent impediment in trench or on roads by night. They ran in the most unexpected fashion and at any height; and when broken, trailed and caught on any jutting thing, to the great misery of hurrying men.'* (Jones)

gooseberries *'arrangement of barbed wire hoops, fastened together to form skeleton sphere, the barbs thrusting outward at every angle.'* (Jones)

39 **picket-irons** *'twisted iron stakes used in construction of wire defences.'* (Jones)

40 **transfigure** In the Bible, Mark 9:3 describes the transfiguration of Jesus: 'And his raiment [clothes] became shining, exceeding white as snow; so as no fuller on earth can white them.'

42 **to play with** *'cf. song: Loola loola loola loola Bye-bye,/ I want the moon to play with/ And the stars to run away with.'* (Jones)

51 **cadency** musical pattern or rhythm.

61 **china** Cockney rhyming slang: 'china plate' means 'mate'.

73–4 *Wigmore* and *Woofferton* are places in the Welsh border country. *Elfael* and *Ceri* are old names for places in Wales. For the Border soldiers waiting to be relieved, the Welsh regiment are *gospelled* because they bring salvation.

76 **marionette** This word begins an extended metaphor comparing the scene to a puppet show or stage performance.

85 **proscenium** front of a stage.

Under Fire: Henri Barbusse

The French novelist Henri Barbusse was already 41 and an established writer when he volunteered in the French army in 1914. Although he initially held an idealized view of the war, he soon lost this while serving as an ordinary soldier and stretcher-bearer on the Western Front. Conditions were atrocious and half the men in his unit were killed in four days. He wrote the novel *Le Feu* (translated as *Under Fire*) during 1915, with the intention of portraying a squad of soldiers as real human beings, rather than perpetuating the idealized view of men in uniform portrayed in propaganda. Although it is based in part on Barbusse's own diaries, the book was criticized for not being factually accurate. Instead, it offers a series of 'visions' and sketches – alternating between brutally realistic close-up details of the soldiers' lives and aerial views of the war on a large scale – which have a mystical or mythological quality.

The book has a clear moral message. By the end, the surviving soldiers feel the war to be 'stupid' and without meaning. They hope to remember and bear witness to what they have suffered, determined that 'There must be no more wars after this one.'

In showing the suffering of the soldiers, even presenting them as martyrs rather than unreal, heroic figures, *Under Fire* was very different from most literature published in the middle of the war. It was widely read and acclaimed, and its influence is recognizable in the work of Siegfried Sassoon and Wilfred Owen, who read the English translation issued in 1917. (See, for example, pages 52–57.)

What questions does Barbusse raise in this extract about the role of religion in the war?

16 **aviator**   aeroplane pilot.
20 ***Gott mit uns!***   God with us!
21 **Zouave**   member of an infantry regiment from French North Africa.
50 *chasseur*   member of French light infantry or light cavalry, trained for rapid action.

Notes

Letter to Susan Owen: **Wilfred Owen**

Wilfred Owen (1893–1918) was one of the greatest poets of the war and is considered by some to be the best war poet of all time. Owen had been planning and practising to be a poet since his boyhood, modelling himself on his hero, the Romantic poet John Keats. He joined the Artists' Rifles late in 1915, trained to become an officer, and joined the Manchester Regiment on the Western Front in January 1917.

He was only at the Front for a few weeks before he was injured. He was invalided home also suffering from shell shock and was sent to Craiglockhart, an army mental hospital, where he met Siegfried Sassoon (see page 118) who encouraged him to write poems that dealt realistically with his experience.

At the Front, in bitterly cold, wet weather, his regiment had orders to reconnoitre and gain ground in preparation for the Battle of Arras, which followed in April. Here, he struggles to find a sufficiently powerful way to put his experience into words in a letter to his mother. Not even the worst traditional images of hell that he can think of – Sodom and Gomorrah, or the Slough of Despond – come close. After less than three weeks in France, the anger that he would later express more fully in his poetry begins to surface, in comments about politicians and attitudes in Britain.

- 12 **GAS**   As he explains, this was *only tear-gas*, frightening enough, but not like the deadly gas attack he was to describe later in his famous poem *Dulce et Decorum Est*.
- 33 **Gramophone**   old-style record player. This would have been a wind-up model.
- 35 **Blighty**   Britain (soldiers' slang.)
- 36 **parvenus**   upstarts; those who have recently risen to power and may not be worthy of it. Lloyd George had become Prime Minister in December 1916.
- 40 **eternal place of gnashing of teeth**   hell.
- 41 **Slough of Despond**   In John Bunyan's morality tale *The Pilgrim's Progress* (1677–8), this is a place of utter despair that

Christian has to pass through on his journey from the City of Destruction. A *slough* is a marsh or mud-filled hole.

42 **Sodom and Gomorrah** In the Old Testament, these cities were places of great evil and sexual depravity. As a punishment, God destroyed them by a rain of burning sulphur – 'brimstone and fire from the Lord out of heaven' (Genesis 19:24).

43 **Babylon** This was another Old Testament city that had fallen out of favour with God.

48–9 **'Somme Pictures', exhibition in Kensington** Unrealistic photographs were released by the army and published by the press, and perfect 'model' trenches had been dug in London, to reassure civilians about conditions at the Front.

54 **Krupp** The Krupp family owned the huge company that manufactured armaments in Germany during the war.

55 **Chlorina Phosgena** Chlorine and phosgene were two forms of poison gas used in the war.

60 **agitate** stir up public protest (against the war).
agitated upset, disturbed.

61 **ague** feverish shivering.

Outline: Paul Nash

Paul Nash (1889–1946) studied for a time at the Slade School of Art and was establishing his career as an artist when war broke out. He enlisted rather reluctantly and served as an infantry officer near Ypres for a few months in 1917. He was injured and returned home, where he exhibited some war drawings which earned him a position as an 'official war artist'. According to Simon Grant, writing in *Tate Magazine* in 2003, the influential artist and critic Roger Fry told Nash: 'I think you have a very special talent for recording a certain poetical aspect of such scenes in a way that no other artist could.'

Nash wrote this letter to his wife during his first tour of duty; in a later letter to her, his description of the landscape becomes much more bleak and he declares that he no longer sees the war from the perspective of a curious artist, but has become:

Notes

> a messenger who will bring back word from the men who are fighting to those who want the war to go on for ever. Feeble, inarticulate, will be my message, but it will have a bitter truth, and may it burn their lousy souls.

Later, he entitled a show of his war paintings 'Void', as if, Grant suggests, it were 'an exhibition about the end of mankind'.

> 30 **the old elements** nature's elements – the seasons and the weather.

Counter-Attack: Siegfried Sassoon

Siegfried Sassoon is a central figure in the literature of the First World War. He knew and influenced several other poets, including Robert Graves and Edmund Blunden, and played a vital role in encouraging Wilfred Owen to write realistically about the war.

His autobiographical writings – in his diaries, his semi-fictional 'Sherston' trilogy and his later memoirs – trace his development from an innocent young English gentleman, immersed in an idyllic life of fox-hunting and sport, who wrote rather mediocre verse in the Georgian manner, into an officer who earned the Military Cross but became fiercely critical of the war. He made his views known in a famous public protest (see page 6) and in his poetry, which was realistic about the horrors of war, and often bitter and satirical.

The poems here are from *The Counter-Attack and Other Poems*, published in 1918. Robert Nichols, another poet, tells us in the introduction to a later edition that Sassoon's bitter poetry had become popular with the soldiers fighting in France, who told him: 'That's the stuff we want. We're fed up with the old men's death-or-glory stunt.'

> 2 **dawn** Descriptions of dawn appear frequently in First World War writing. Some writers contrast the beauty of dawn with their grim surroundings, but often the coming light has a bleak or even sinister quality. There are several examples in Barbusse's *Under Fire*; see also *Exposure* by Wilfred Owen,

page 54. Notice the simile Sassoon has chosen here, which conveys both the appearance of the dawn and the feelings of the soldiers.
13 **jolly old rain!**   What is the effect of this phrase? It sounds out of place in the midst of this grim description. Some critics suggest it is satirical, others that it is an attempt to capture the stoical nonchalance of the soldiers.
17 **five-nines**   a type of shell.

Dreamers: Siegfried Sassoon

This is another poem from *The Counter-Attack* (see above). Here Sassoon uses a series of contrasts to convey the reality of what it means to be a soldier. Caught up in a generalized *hour of destiny* (3), they remain individuals with their own hopes and fears, longing now for the ordinary life that they may previously have taken for granted.

13 **spats**   covers made of stiff fabric, extending from the top of the shoe to the lower leg, that were fashionable in the late nineteenth and early twentieth century.

Exposure: Wilfred Owen

On 6 April 1917, Wilfred Owen (see also page 116) wrote in a letter to his mother that 'We stuck to our line 4 days (and 4 nights) without relief, in the open, and in the snow'. The terrible tension of being trapped in a state of enforced inactivity, exposed to the elements and simultaneously to constant uncertainty and fear of possible attack and sudden death, is powerfully and brilliantly evoked in this poem, which was written the following year. The poem, originally entitled *Nothing Happens*, charts one cycle of night, through day and back to night, in which the soldiers can do little but wait.

A feature of Owen's work is his use of 'pararhyme', a form of rhyme where the consonants of the relevant syllable are the same, but the vowel sounds are not (for example, *burn* and *born* in stanza 7). This type of rhyme can bring about a subtle feeling of unease.

Notes

In *Exposure*, we see Owen at the height of his powers, using pararhyme and aural imagery with the assurance of a musical virtuoso. Look carefully at the sheer variety of sound effects – alliteration, assonance, and internal rhyme – built into almost every line. Consider also the pace of the poem, and the cumulative effect created by the short line at the end of each stanza.

- 1 Owen ironically echoes the opening of Keats's *Ode to a Nightingale*: 'My heart aches, and a drowsy numbness pains/ My sense'.
- 3 **salient** a place where the front line jutted into enemy territory, where fighting would be fierce and defence particularly important.
- 14 **grey** German uniforms were grey, and the Germans approached from *the east* (13). However, the grey clouds, bringing snow and rain, seem even more threatening to life and morale than the enemy.
- 23 **drowse** This is perhaps another echo of Keats (see Note to line 1). The soldiers, lying in the snow, dream of life at home in an idealized English countryside of *blossoms* and *blackbird* (24), and seem to be falling into the dangerously drowsy state of hypothermia.
- 26–30 Compare the words of the popular song 'Keep the home fires burning... Though your lads are far away they dream of home'. But dreaming of home brings no comfort. This stanza suggests that if the men did return to their homes, they would find them abandoned, and that the doors would be closed against them. The repetition emphasizes the feeling that they have been shut out – they have been sent to the Front and are expected to stay there. Reluctantly they *turn back* to reality.
- 31–5 The soldiers have to try to hold on to the belief that they are fighting for something worthwhile. They suffer willingly, in order to preserve *kind fires* and truth and freedom for their children. Like Christ, they feel they were born to be sacrificed for others.
- 34 **loath** unwilling, reluctant.
- 35 This line can be interpreted as meaning either that their suffering is so great because God no longer loves them, or the

inhumanity of the war shows that humans have ceased to love God.

36–40 Notice the devastating effect of this final stanza. The eyes of both living and dead *are ice*.

The Show: Wilfred Owen

See the headnote on page 116 for information on Wilfred Owen. This relentlessly bleak poem presents a grim, aerial view of a battle on the Western Front. Accompanied by the personification of Death, the narrator's soul surveys the scene from a height. He describes a grotesque, diseased landscape in which lines of advancing troops, which look from above like long caterpillars writhing in agony, destroy and 'eat' each other. Finally, he falls to earth, where Death shows him one of the 'worms' with its head severed. This proves to be his own head. Commanding his platoon, Owen would have been literally at its head during single-file advances.

Initially entitled *Vision*, the poem was drafted in November 1917, when Owen had recently been 'set alight' by the prize-winning war novel *Under Fire*, by the French writer Henri Barbusse (see pages 44 and 115); its first chapter is entitled 'The Vision' and includes similar bird's-eye images of the trenches.

This may have been the first time Owen made consistent and effective use of pararhyme (see page 119) in his war poetry. In a letter to Siegfried Sassoon he asks, 'What do you think of my Vowel-rime stunt, in this [À *Terre*] and "Vision"?'

Title During the First World War, 'show' was soldiers' slang for battle. Here, the narrator sees the battle from a distance, as if watching a performance. The quotation from W.B. Yeats's poetic drama *The Shadowy Waters* (1906) is used ironically, with the word *tarnished* in place of the original *burnished*. It refers to *ever-living* gods who create humans then indifferently watch their suffering.

3–5 Compare Owen's use of language in his letter of 19 January 1917 (page 48), where he describes the appearance of No Man's

Notes

> Land. The desolation is so great that he struggles to find images strong enough to convey the horror of it.

3 **dearth** famine. The barren landscape is sick and feverish as if from starvation.

6 **beard... wire** the coils of barbed wire used as barricades at the Front.

17 **Brown... grey** The British troops wear khaki, the Germans grey. The *bristling spines* are the spiked helmets of the Germans.

18 The *caterpillars* – or troops – have come from *green* countryside; it seems unnatural that they should be so *intent* on coming into this sick landscape of mud.

19 **spawns** The German troops appear to multiply more quickly – like fish or frogs producing masses of eggs.

20 **Ramped** as in 'rampaged': attacked with violent aggression.

Casualties of war

Non-Combatants and Others: Rose Macaulay

Rose Macaulay had already written seven novels when the war began. She wished to be involved along with the men, but a few months' service as a VAD, nursing the wounded, was enough to destroy her romantic illusions about the fighting, and prompted the writing of *Non-Combatants and Others* in 1916.

The writer of a novel in the middle of the war was faced with the difficulty of imposing a conventional narrative structure on events that seemed to offer no hope of ending or resolution. However, Macaulay deliberately takes on this sense of meaninglessness and endlessness in the theme and structure of *Non-Combatants and Others*. It ends with a series of short vignettes showing how various characters, combatants and non-combatants, spend New Year's Eve, 1915, and a final inconclusive remark: 'The year of grace 1915 slipped away into darkness, like a broken ship drifting on bitter tides on to a waste shore. The next year began.'

The novel follows the experience of a young woman, Alix

Sandomir, who comes to feel and recognize the truth about war through witnessing the effects it has on the men around her. She becomes a committed pacifist.

Here, at the novel's climax, Alix is out for a walk with chance acquaintances and accidentally learns the truth about the death of her 18-year-old brother Paul. Earlier, relatives have assured her that 'He died a noble death… serving his country in her need.'

This is one of the earliest fictional accounts of a self-inflicted wound, a theme that became common in later war writings.

- 4 **pug**   small breed of dog, sometimes used as a mascot.
- 18–19 **whizz-bangs**   shells fired from light or field artillery. They travelled faster than the speed of sound, so the 'whizz' of the shell would be heard or felt before the 'bang' of the gun that fired it, giving soldiers no time to react.
- 50 **Ancient Mariner**   In Coleridge's famous poem *The Rime of the Ancient Mariner*, an old sailor is forced, in order to expiate his guilt, to wander the earth telling all who will listen the tale of how he brought bad luck to his ship by killing an albatross. Macaulay suggests that this young man is similarly obsessive in his need to talk about his experience.

Journey's End: R.C. Sherriff

R.C. Sherriff (1896–1975) served as a captain in the East Surrey regiment for most of the war. He was not a professional writer, and initially wrote *Journey's End* for an amateur dramatic society. It became a hit after a one-off performance with Laurence Olivier playing the lead role. Although it is not considered to be a great play, and the characters are rather stereotypical, it works well on the stage, and soldier audiences responded to it with enthusiasm.

It is realistic, and set entirely in a British dug-out just before the German offensive of March 1918. This extract raises the issue of cowardice, but Sherriff avoids the full implications of this by making Hibbert rather miraculously recover his nerve in time for the final attack. Where do your sympathies lie in response to the dialogue here?

> 4 **neuralgia** pain originating in the nerves, which is notoriously difficult to diagnose or treat as it often has no obvious external cause.

The New Book of Martyrs: Georges Duhamel

Georges Duhamel (1884–1966) was a French doctor and author who joined up and served as a surgeon with the French army throughout the war. He often worked in dangerous conditions and he witnessed a great deal of suffering, which moved him deeply. In response, he wrote *La Vie des Martyrs* (translated as *The New Book of Martyrs*), a harrowing series of observations of injured and dying men. The book was published in France in 1917, and like Henri Barbusse's *Under Fire* (see page 44) it became popular with British readers, contributing to the change of opinions in the last years of the war. Siegfried Sassoon acknowledged its influence in his diary.

The choice of the word *Martyrs* in the title is revealing. Duhamel was not interested in the war as such, but only in the men who came under his care. His intention was to portray and commemorate soldiers not as heroes, but as victims of the war who had been irrevocably changed by their experiences. His final words, addressed to the reader, tell us that he felt it was not enough just to be a skilful doctor. It was also his mission to 'record the history of those who have been the sacrificial victims of the race, without gloss, in all its truth and simplicity'.

In this extract, Duhamel records the struggle between the forces of life and nature and those of death and despair, as a young man faces a life of disability.

Disabled: Wilfred Owen

Here Wilfred Owen (see page 116) creates a compassionate portrait of a terribly disabled young soldier, left sitting in his wheelchair while life goes on around him. A good-looking footballer, he had been flattered into joining the army without any real understanding of the possible consequences. Now, though, he is horribly mutilated, and people turn away from him in embarrassment. Formerly fit and virile, he is now utterly dependent on others. He takes what little pity and charity he can get, waiting helplessly in the cold for the nurses to come and put him to bed.

- 2 **ghastly suit of grey** ugly hospital uniform, or cheap civilian suit – very different from his colourful regimental tartan.
- 7 **Town** This is likely to be Edinburgh. Owen was familiar with the city during his time at Craiglockhart (see page 116).
- 8 Perhaps there is a suggestion of the gas-lamps being lit among the trees in the blue light of dusk, possibly in Princes Street Gardens, in the centre of Edinburgh.
- 14–15 He was so handsome that an artist had been desperate to paint his portrait.
- 19 **half his lifetime lapsed** It was as if while he lay bleeding from his wound, he aged rapidly – half of his life was taken away.
- 20 **spurted** The spurting blood perhaps ironically suggests the sexual ejaculation no longer possible for him.
- 21–2 He was a hero of his football team, and saw a smear of blood on his leg as a badge of his virility and prowess.
- 23 **a peg** a drink, probably of whisky or brandy. He was flattered into joining up when he was a little drunk.
- 25 **kilts** As a member of a Scottish regiment, he would have worn the full Highland dress: the kilt in the regimental tartan, with his skean-dhu, or dagger, tucked into his matching socks.
- 27 **giddy jilts** flirtatious, capricious young women.
- 29 **lie** He pretended to be over 18, in order to be accepted for military service.
- 32–3 **jewelled hilts… plaid socks** See Note to line 25.
- 35 *Esprit de corps* team spirit. Perhaps he imagined it to be like that of his football team.
- 38–9 The only person who shows interest is a parson or chaplain doing his charitable duty.
- 45–6 Now completely dependent, he helplessly waits for nurses to come and put him to bed.

Notes

Non-combatants

My Heart's Right There: Florence L. Barclay

Although it is not great literature, this extract captures the mood of early-war writing and shows a highly conventional and idealized view of what was expected of patriotic men and women of the time. Florence Barclay (1862–1921) came from a religious family and became a rector's wife. During a spell of ill-health, she began writing romantic novels and stories to pass the time. Her second novel, *The Rosary*, became a runaway best-seller in 1910, but her work is now largely forgotten.

My Heart's Right There is a patriotic, pro-war story in which a young soldier goes to fight in France, leaving his wife and child behind. He is wounded and returns home for a while, tells her about his experiences, but then returns to the Front. It illustrates the traditional role of women, who were expected to be passive, to 'keep the home fires burning', to worry and to wait.

The title comes from the music hall song, 'It's a Long Way to Tipperary', which became one of the most popular marching songs for British troops in the First World War. The chorus aptly sums up the sentiment of Barclay's story:

> It's a long way to Tipperary
> To the sweetest girl I know!
> Goodbye Piccadilly,
> Farewell Leicester Square!
> It's a long long way to Tipperary,
> But my heart's right there.

Non-Combatant: Cicely Hamilton

A prominent suffragette, Cicely Hamilton (1872–1952) was not comfortable with the traditional woman's passive, non-combatant role in the war. She was a successful actor and writer as well as a dedicated feminist, and in 1908 co-founded the Women Writers' Suffrage League, for which she wrote campaigning literature.

During the war she worked in a hospital in France, became an army auxiliary and also created a theatre company to help entertain the troops. Here she forcefully expresses rage and frustration that women's abilities and energy were being wasted. She is perhaps most concerned with the 'women's war' for equality.

A Journal of Impressions in Belgium: May Sinclair

May Sinclair, a successful novelist in her fifties, was keen to play a part in the war. At the end of September 1914, she volunteered with a British Red Cross ambulance unit in Belgium. She was secretary and treasurer to the unit, but hoped to be involved in nursing and to write articles for *The Daily Chronicle*. However, as a woman, her efforts to become fully involved were not welcomed and she was forced to return home after a few months. This record of her experiences was described by the writer Rebecca West as a 'gallant, humiliated book'.

1 **Taube** airship.

Mr Britling Sees It Through: H.G. Wells

H.G. Wells is now most famous for his science fiction novels, such as *The Time Machine* and *The War of the Worlds*, but he also wrote about history and politics. He became a committed socialist and pacifist.

The central character in *Mr Britling Sees It Through* (1916) is Hugh Britling, a middle-class, middle-aged journalist, and perhaps also, as his name suggests, a representative 'little' or ordinary Briton. The novel follows him from the outbreak of war, when it seems like a 'splendid dream', through his gradual disillusionment until late in 1915 when his son is killed and he almost sinks into despair. It captured the mood of those on the home front and soldiers appreciated it too. Siegfried Sassoon wrote that he devoured its pages 'in a rapt surrender of attention'.

The extract here contains an account of a Zeppelin airship raid on the east coast of England. Several resorts on the east coast,

Notes

including Scarborough and Great Yarmouth, were attacked by Zeppelins during the first year of the war, causing the deaths of civilians, including children.

> 3 **watering-place** seaside resort or spa town where people went for the sake of their health.
> 40 **Jules Verne** French author of early science fiction stories.
> 49 **Emperor Patience** a complex version of the patience or solitaire card game, named after Napoleon, who was – incorrectly – thought to have amused himself by playing patience while exiled on the island of St Helena.
> 50 **Potsdam creature** the Kaiser, or German emperor.

Armistice

'And There Was a Great Calm': Thomas Hardy

Although we saw earlier (page 105) that Thomas Hardy did contribute to the propaganda effort in 1914, this did not reflect his attitude to war in general. He was always somewhat melancholy, aware of irony, and tended to question whether there was meaning in life; the brutality of the war increased his pessimism. In her biography, *The Early Life of Thomas Hardy, 1840–1891*, his wife Florence suggests that the war 'destroyed all Hardy's belief in the gradual ennoblement of man' and 'gave the *coup de grâce* to any conception he may have nourished of a fundamental ultimate Wisdom at the back of things'. (See also Note to lines 21–2 below.)

This poem was written in 1918 at the time of the Armistice, and published in 1922 in *Late Lyrics and Earlier*. In it we hear the signals that mark the coming of peace, but there is no celebration, only an unnatural feeling of calm. After reminding us of all the anguish and devastation, Hardy leaves us with only the bitter, unanswered and unanswerable question of why the war took place at all.

Notice the mixture of language here: archaic vocabulary and religious references appear alongside colloquial language and details specific to the war. The 'spirits' of *Pity* and *Irony* also appear in the chorus of Hardy's epic verse drama *The Dynasts*.

- Title   This is a quotation from the Bible, Matthew 8:26. During a storm at sea, when the men of little faith trembled, Christ 'arose, and rebuked the winds and the sea; and there was a great calm'.
- 1–5   How has Hardy summed up the experience of the war here?
- 17–18   **Sirius… flapping**   Sirius, or the Dog Star, is the brightest star in the sky. Hardy suggests that it seemed to stop twinkling.
- 19   **boom**   As Vera Brittain explains in the next extract (page 82), maroons (flares fired from mortars) were set off to mark the signing of the Armistice. Hardy may be referring to this, but here he suggests the signal is not clear; it sounds muffled and distant. He may therefore be describing the sound of the guns in France, which could sometimes be heard or felt on the other side of the English Channel.
- 21–2   **when old hopes… dead and damned**   Hardy shared the common feeling that the war destroyed any belief that human civilization was advancing in a positive way.
- 23–5   **Said the bereft… used to run?**   Similarly, the *meek, and lowly* ask whether the human race will be blessed and reach a state of *grace*, as they used to believe. Hardy suggests that such religious beliefs were *dreams*, and the question is not answered. Notice the religious vocabulary.
- 25   **sooth**   truth, reality (archaic).
- 35   **peradventures**   challenges, contests (an unusual archaic usage).
- 36–40   There are no humans in this stanza. How does Hardy describe the impact of the sudden peace on the natural world?
- 41   **clemency**   mercy, forgiveness.
- 42   In the Bible, Luke 2 describes the annunciation to the shepherds of the birth of Christ. Angels appear in the sky singing and proclaiming *peace on earth*. As well as the obvious point that the guns are now silent, Hardy may be referring once more to a loss of religious faith: there are no angels, only *silence in the sky*.

Testament of Youth: Vera Brittain

See the headnote on page 104 for information on Vera Brittain. Her war memoir was published in 1933; she describes it as an attempt to 'tell history in terms of personal life' and to come to

Notes

terms with her war experience and the loss of her companions.

Although there was jubilation when the war finally ended, quite a few accounts by those who had fought or suffered report not joy but the kind of numbness described here. Siegfried Sassoon, for example, writes in *Siegfried's Journey* that his mind was 'blank' and that he observed the celebrations rather than sharing them.

Look at the extract from Vera Brittain's diary on page 16 and compare the tone and style of her reflections.

- 6 **maroons** mortar guns blasted flares, or maroons, into the air to mark the signing of the Armistice.
- 18 **Occasional Oratorio** An oratorio is a piece of dramatic music for singers and orchestra, usually on a religious theme. However, this example was composed in 1746 to commemorate the English victory over the Scots at the Battle of Culloden.
- 40 **Edward** Vera Brittain's younger brother, who died on active service in Italy.
- 41 **Roland** Vera Brittain's fiancé, who was killed in December 1915 (see pages 109–110).
- 93 **Victor and Geoffrey** close friends of Roland, Vera and Edward.

Now It Can Be Told: Philip Gibbs

Philip Gibbs (1877–1962) wrote about the war from two very different viewpoints. He was a journalist with the *Daily Mail*, and at the outbreak of war he went to work on the Western Front as a reporter, but was arrested and sent home for refusing to comply with the demands of the censors. Soon afterwards, he was offered the opportunity to become an official reporter. He did so, and despite his frustration, he agreed to write articles that followed the official line and suited the requirements of the censors for the remainder of the war. However, once the war was over and censorship lifted, he wrote the book *The Realities of War*, published in the US as *Now It Can Be Told* (1920), a much more honest and realistic account of what he had witnessed. The book's purpose, he wrote in its Preface, was 'to get deeper to the truth of this war and of all war' in the hope of improving international relations and preventing 'another massacre of youth like that five years' sacrifice of boys of which I was a witness'.

In this extract, he exposes the reality of what awaited the returning war 'heroes'. It is poignant to compare this and Wilfred Owen's *Disabled* (page 66) with the doctor's promises in the scene from Georges Duhamel's *New Book of Martyrs* (page 63).

Title Published in the UK as *The Realities of War*. The title used for the American edition, *Now It Can Be Told*, reveals clearly that Gibbs felt he had not previously been free to tell the truth.
   32 **The girls were clinging to their jobs**   Women had been taken on to fill many of the vacancies, not just in factories and munitions work, but in other workplaces too, while the men were at the Front. For example, the number of women working in banking rose from under 10,000 to over 60,000, while around 100,000 more became bus conductors.

Later perspectives on the war

Parade's End: Ford Madox Ford

Ford (born Ford Hermann Hueffer in 1873) was a key figure in the arts before the war. He was editor of *The English Review*, and encouraged and worked with many well-known writers. He was excited by new modernist and experimental ideas that were emerging just before the war. Although he was over military age when war broke out, he joined the Welsh Regiment before going to France, where he served for a time as a transport officer. He was wounded and returned home in 1917 suffering from shell shock and amnesia as well as lung damage.

Some of his experiences provided material for *Parade's End*, which was published during the 1920s. It is a vast novel in four parts and explores the experience and effects of the war within the wider context of history. It follows a central character, Christopher Tietjens, through the years before the war, on active

Notes

service in France, and his efforts to find a way to live afterwards. As Samuel Hynes puts it in *A War Imagined: The First World War and English Culture* (1990), *Parade's End* is 'a novel that begins in the ostensible security of pre-war England and moves through the dispersals and destructions of the war to end in the fragmented, disoriented post-war world'.

Regarded as one of the great novels to come out of the war, it is written in an impressionistic, modernist style. This extract from the second part, *No More Parades*, portrays in a humorous, ironic way the tensions between different ranks, officers and senior staff. Tietjens has the job of organizing and equipping new drafts of men before they go to the front line. He is under pressure, but hampered by bureaucracy; one of his men has just been killed; the last thing he needs is a visit from the staff colonel.

- 5 **G.S.O.II** General Staff Officer, Grade 2. Staff officers worked behind the lines and did not engage in combat.
- 12 **orfcers** The sergeant-major has a Cockney accent. Here and elsewhere, Ford differentiates between social classes by their modes of speech. Look for other examples. How does this add to the effectiveness of the text?
- 15 **staffwallah** In this context, the term is not very respectful in tone; it means something like 'that staff fellow'. (Wallah is from a Hindu word meaning a person connected with a job or function, such as a kitchen-wallah, or a rickshaw-wallah, in India.)
- 26 **strafed** This usually means to be attacked with bombs or machine-gun fire from low-flying aircraft; here, it is probably hyperbole, meaning they expect a good telling off or punishment.
- 32 **cavalry gadgets** fancy epaulettes.
- 40 **shopwalker** senior sales assistant in a department store.
- 72 **drawing** requisitioning or ordering equipment from the army stores. This would have involved paperwork and bureaucracy.
- 76 **tin-hats** The man died because they had not been able to obtain proper protective equipment.
- 87–8 **Colonial troops… from the Dominions** Canada had ceased to be a British colony, gained 'dominion' status and become self-governing in 1867; this status was formalized, along with that of

Australia and New Zealand, after the Boer War in 1907. The colonel reveals that he is behind the times in his thinking.

Oh What a Lovely War: Theatre Workshop

By the 1960s, when there were fewer survivors of the war still alive, it became possible to use the war as a subject for black comedy or satire. *Oh What a Lovely War*, first staged in 1963, is a musical show or revue that depicts the war satirically, though its intention was still to highlight the horror of war. It is designed to be performed by a troop of *pierrots*, or live 'puppets', and makes use of songs, dance and projector slides, as well as dialogue.

The extract is from near the end of the show – and of the war – when the long stalemate of trench warfare is about to be ended by the arrival of American troops. Various characters are on 'Sunday parade', where their 'prayers' reveal a variety of attitudes.

What is suggested about the role of religion during the war? Compare this with the beginning of the extract by R.H. Tawney (page 36) and with Henri Barbusse's *Under Fire* (page 44).

    6 **'When this lousy war is over'** The versions of songs included here were popular with soldiers in the trenches.

15–16 **O Lord… thy word** These words are from the *Nunc Dimittis*, or the *Song of Simeon*, a canticle based on Luke 2:29–32, which forms part of the liturgy for evening or night prayers in the Christian tradition. It is ironic here as Simeon, an old man, had been promised that he would not die until he saw the Saviour. He spoke these words when Mary and Joseph brought the baby Jesus to him, saying that he was now ready to die.

23–4 This is the opening of *The Children's Song* by Rudyard Kipling, which became a popular hymn and was often sung in schools.

   38 **cleanly** This is an ironic word for men in the trenches.

MCMXIV: Philip Larkin

In this poem Philip Larkin (1922–1985) looks back with hindsight on the *innocence* (32) of 1914. The descriptions in the poem suggest it is responding to an old photograph of men

Notes

queuing to join up, or commenting on a series of images the poet has seen. The poem evokes a sense of the past, and of a very different way of life that vanished with the war. It was first published in Larkin's collection *The Whitsun Weddings* in 1964.

- Title These are the Roman numerals for 1914. The date often appears in this form on war memorials.
- 4 *The Oval* is an international cricket ground in London; *Villa Park* is the home stadium of Aston Villa football club, in the West Midlands. This echoes the link between soldiering and sport that appears frequently in early war texts.
- 11 **farthings and sovereigns** obsolete British coins that were current in 1914. A farthing, worth 1/4 penny, was then the smallest coin; a sovereign was a gold coin worth £1.
- 15 **twist** tobacco that could be chewed or smoked in a pipe.
- 20 **Domesday lines** The Domesday Book was a great survey of England completed in 1086 for William the Conqueror. It recorded how the land was broken down into estates, who owned it, and how much it was worth. Larkin is suggesting that in 1914 rural England was still roughly based on the old divisions laid down in the eleventh century.

Strange Meeting: Susan Hill

Susan Hill (born in 1942) tells us in the Afterword to her novel that it grew out of an 'obsession' with the First World War that 'haunted' her as a young adult. Although she was fascinated by Wilfred Owen and the other poets, she says, her own book is fictional. It is not based on the life of any individual soldier, although she drew 'hints' from biographies, memoirs and letters.

In contrast to Ford's huge, panoramic *Parade's End* (see page 87), she chose to write 'a novel of the war in microcosm, to create a small world within the great one of the whole war'. The book focuses on a few months in the life of John Hilliard, a young subaltern, and his friendship with a new young officer, David Barton.

In this extract, Hilliard has just returned to the Western Front after sick leave in England, where no one had any real understanding of the horrors of the war. A major offensive has been raging, and he finds his battalion tragically altered.

> Title This refers to one of Wilfred Owen's best-known poems, *Strange Meeting*, which portrays a fantasy encounter between a soldier and an 'enemy' he has killed. The waste and pointlessness of war is summed up in the line 'I am the enemy you killed, my friend.' (See the Oxford Student Texts edition of *Wilfred Owen: Selected Poems and Letters*, OUP, 2009.)
> 34 **Mons, Le Cateau and Ypres**   These were major battles on the Western Front. Battles occurred at Mons and Le Cateau in August 1914; five battles took place in the vicinity of Ypres at different stages in the war.

Observe the Sons of Ulster Marching Towards the Somme: Frank McGuinness

This play by the award-winning Irish playwright and poet Frank McGuinness (born in 1953) was first produced in 1985 and has won many awards. It focuses on the experience of eight men who volunteer to serve in the 36th (Ulster) Division at the beginning of the war, but explores this in relation to the longstanding troubles over religious divisions and Irish home rule.

Ulster was the Northern province of Ireland, which was then under British rule. Unionists, or Loyalists, who supported the union with Britain and were mainly Protestant, clashed with Nationalists, who were mainly Catholic and wanted home rule for Ireland. Matters were coming to a head in April 1914, but the First World War interrupted the hostilities. Thousands of Ulstermen and Irishmen of all religions and sects volunteered to fight, and died. The 36th (Ulster) Division suffered particularly heavy casualties. In the Battle of the Somme, over 6,000 members of the Division were killed in a single day, and entire villages were left without young men because of a policy of grouping recruits with neighbours from their own communities.

The eight characters in the play are all Protestant Unionists,

Notes

but they have very different backgrounds and attitudes, and conflicts arise between them. However, in the stress of war, the men bond with each other. The extract is from the climax as the characters wait to go 'over the top' into the Battle of the Somme.

71 **Fenians**   The Fenian Brotherhood was an organization dedicated to the establishment of an independent Irish Republic in the nineteenth and early twentieth century. The original meaning has expanded to include all supporters of Irish nationalism, and it is also sometimes used as a disparaging term for Irish Catholics.

Waiting for the Telegram: Alan Bennett

The prolific author and playwright Alan Bennett was born in Yorkshire in 1934. *Talking Heads* is an acclaimed series of dramatic monologues written for television, each starring a single actor. They are studies of people who are eccentric, or who live on the margins of society, and they explore themes such as loneliness and guilt. The monologues make effective use of subtexts: the characters often reveal a great deal more about themselves and their attitudes and motivation than they intend.

Waiting for the Telegram is from the second series, first broadcast in 1998, and featured Dame Thora Hird, who won a BAFTA Best Actress award for her performance.

Violet, the speaker here, is nearing her 100th birthday. She has had a stroke, which has affected her memory for words. Throughout this moving monologue, she sits in a wheelchair in a nursing home. Verity and Francis are among the workers who care for her. She is expecting a telegram from the Queen on her birthday, but here she remembers the arrival of a different sort of telegram. Despite her difficulty with words, once she gets in touch with her memories of the distant past Violet's thoughts and feelings are expressed more fluently, and we learn that she has spent much of her long and largely unhappy life regretting the decision she made not to have sex with her lover just before he went to his death in the First World War.

Interpretations

This section contains activities and critical commentary, and is designed to stimulate discussion of the texts and to encourage you to draw comparisons between them.

Developing an awareness of how attitudes to the war changed over time is a key aspect of the study of First World War literature. The first part of this section, Language, Style and Attitude, focuses on these changes and on how they are reflected in the content, language and style of the texts. The second part, Contrasts and Conflicts, explores a range of other topics and themes that are typical of First World War literature. The final part, Aftermath, looks at reflections on the end of the war.

Of course, it is possible to approach the texts in different ways, and there are many useful links to be drawn between them. As you work with the texts, you may find it helpful to make notes about other interesting points of comparison and contrast that occur to you.

Language, style and attitude

'Clarion call'

Immediately war was declared, writers responded with a flood of patriotic literature. Journalists and essay writers rushed to express their views, and huge numbers of poems were written. During the month of August 1914, about 100 poems were submitted to *The Times* every day, for example. Most of these were not very good: they were fervent, but clichéd expressions of support for the war, mainly written by those who did not have to take part. Within weeks, Charles F.G. Masterman, who headed the new War Propaganda Bureau, had called together a large group of well-known, respected authors, such as G.K. Chesterton, Arthur Conan Doyle and Thomas Hardy, and asked

Interpretations

them to help in convincing the public that this was a 'righteous war'. As noted on page 105, Hardy's poem, *Men Who March Away* (page 19) was one product of this meeting.

For these writers, war was not yet a reality, and since they were all older men, for them it never would be. Writing from this initial phase of the war tends to draw on language, concepts and images that belong to a much older vision of war. The Victorians had a fascination with mythology and with the medieval tradition of chivalry, where gallant knights in shining armour rode out on trusty steeds to right the wrongs of the world. This carried over into the traditional war poetry that was written early in the war.

Activity

Read the extract from Vera Brittain's diary on page 16.
- How would you describe the tone or mood of the extract?
- How does Vera Brittain present her own response to the outbreak of war?

Discussion

Although there is confusion and disruption, and although Brittain describes 3 August 1914 as *the blackest Bank Holiday within memory* (lines 16–17), the dominant feeling is of excitement. At first, she uses words such as *thrilling* (2), *stupendous* (34), *remarkable* (35) and *unparalleled* (36) as if in an attempt to grasp the magnitude of the events she is reading about in the newspapers, but as yet there is a sense of unreality. The possible personal impact of the war comes closer when she sees the young woman crying as her husband leaves to go on active service, yet she still describes them as *quite calm* (68). As the days pass, there is a feeling of restlessness and suspense as people seem unsure how to react, and nothing much happens.

Brittain comes across here as intelligent, curious and eager to understand and be involved. She also seems young, naïve and inexperienced. She reads the newspapers and wants to know what is happening, but it is clear that she does so without questioning what she reads. She reports almost casually the incident where she showed her brother an appeal for volunteers to join the army, and he

Language, style and attitude

suddenly got very keen (74), while she herself promptly begins knitting, *the only work it seems possible as yet for women to do* (93–94). If you read this account with hindsight about the war, or already know her story, the innocence of her response seems ironic and painful.

Another influence on early responses to the war was the tradition of the English public school, with its emphasis on keen sportsmanship, playing for the team, and gentlemanly conduct. Religion had a part to play too: God was often invoked as being on 'our side' and the war was frequently described in religious terms. Fighting was a religious duty, and dying a holy sacrifice.

Activity

Read the following extract. It is from the anonymous introduction to a popular anthology of poetry published in 1914, called *Songs and Sonnets for England in Wartime*. *The Call* by R.E. Vernède and *Men Who March Away* by Thomas Hardy were both included in this volume.

> In the stress of a nation's peril some of its greatest songs are born. In the stress of a nation's peril the poet at last comes into his own again, and with clarion call he rouses the sleeping soul of the empire. Prophet he is, champion and consoler.
>
> If in these later times the poet has been neglected, now in our infinite need, in our pride and our sorrow, he is here to strengthen, comfort and inspire. The poet is vindicated.
>
> What can so nobly uplift the hearts of a people facing war with its unspeakable agony as music and poetry? The sound of martial music steels men's hearts before battle. The sound of martial words inspires human souls to do and to endure. God, His poetry, and His music are the Holy Trinity of war.

What does the writer suggest is the job of the war poet? Comment on the style of the language used here.

Interpretations

Discussion

The writer suggests that the role of the traditional war poet is to stir up nationalistic feeling, to encourage or 'champion' the troops of one side, and to console those who suffer or lose loved ones by presenting war as a noble cause.

In this Introduction, the writer refers to the war in old-fashioned religious terms, as if it is some kind of crusade supported by God. Overall, the Introduction is written in elevated language and a rhetorical style, as if the author is making a speech or proclamation. For example the opening phrase of the first two sentences is repeated, there is a rhetorical question, and ideas are grouped in threes, as in 'Prophet he is, champion and consoler'. Archaic vocabulary, such as 'peril' or 'clarion call', which recall the language of medieval chivalry, makes this writing seem remote from real experience.

Activity

Read the poems *The Vigil* by Sir Henry Newbolt (page 15) and *The Call* by R.E. Vernède (page 21).
- What is the purpose of these poems, and how does each writer set out to achieve it?
- What do you notice about each writer's language and imagery?

Discussion

Both poems call on the men of England to be ready to fight for their country. Newbolt urges *England* itself to respond to the *drums* and *trumpets* (27–28) that traditionally signal war, to follow the example of war heroes of the past, who were *Single-hearted, unafraid* (17), and to live up to its past history of *ancient might* (31). Although the poem is addressed to a generalized *England*, the intention is that it would be experienced as a personal challenge by every Englishman.

Vernède, in *The Call*, also addresses the men of England, but in a less abstract way than Newbolt. Stanza by stanza he singles out individuals, or 'types' of men, of varied ages and backgrounds – the sporting public schoolboy, the purposeful, ambitious businessman, the imaginative *Dreamer*, the man who has suffered a hard life, and

Language, style and attitude

the lazy *Lover of ease* – and promises them all, in their own terms, that they will *not regret* (31) choosing to fight. He presents joining up as a rare opportunity to *pass from the common sort/ Sudden and stand by the heroes' side* (43–44).

Newbolt combines traditional war images with an extended metaphor of England as a medieval knight going through his initiation (see Notes page 103). He uses archaic, high-flown language and religious vocabulary. The opening image of the *sacred flame... before the inmost shrine* sets the poem in the reverent atmosphere of a church. The refrain, *Pray that God defend the Right*, assumes England will be fighting a righteous war with the blessing of God. The effect is to give the war an aura of holiness, and to make fighting sound like a religious duty.

Vernède uses a variety of images and ideas as he aligns himself with each of the men he addresses. The young man in the opening stanza, for example, is idealized: good looking, quick and cheerful, his *clear* eyes shine with honesty. The war is compared to sport – it is *the game of games*; it is as if he is being offered the ultimate promotion to the national team, as he is urged to swap his school *blazer and cap* for *England's colours*. In stanza 3, Vernède enters into the fairytale world of the *Dreamer*, and suggests that the war offers a chance for his dreams of smiting *ogres* and rescuing *the fair Princess* to come true. Vernède also uses some archaic and religious language. In the final stanza he claims that the *clarion call* to fight is sounded by Christ himself – the one *who deathless died*.

Although the dominant attitude at the time was pro-war and patriotic, this was not universal. Some writers did challenge the accepted view of the war, but many soon found themselves subject to censorship, which made it difficult to publish their work. Although the poet Isaac Rosenberg fought in the war, he was never in favour of it (see Notes page 106).

Activity
Look at Isaac Rosenberg's poem *On Receiving News of the War*, which was written in 1914, although not published until after his death.

Interpretations

Comment on the ideas, language and imagery in the poem. What sense does it give of Rosenberg's attitude to the war?

Discussion

Here are some of the points you may have noted.
- The poem appears simple, with its short stanzas and regular rhyme, but is quite enigmatic and impressionistic.
- The main image is a metaphor of war as an untimely, icy winter, which has arrived during summer; not only does it affect the land but it is in *all men's hearts* (9).
- War also seems to be an evil (*malign*) spirit that has ruined life (*turned... Our lives to mould*, 11–12) and also a wild beast, with horrific *Red fangs*, which has *torn* the face of God (13).
- God is not seen as a supporter of war here, but as its victim. Human attention is all directed to the war, while God is abandoned and seems to be the only one who *mourns* (15).
- Rosenberg's response is very different from that of the traditional war poets. He is anti-war and foresees the devastating effect it will have. However, the final stanza adds a further idea. Here he seems also to see the possibility that war could have a cleansing effect. By referring to it as the *ancient crimson curse* he suggests it has always been part of human nature. With the powerful, harsh alliteration of the repeated c's, he calls on war to destroy, and *consume*, as if to bring about some kind of rebirth: *Give back this universe/ Its pristine bloom*.

In the years leading up to the war, a small but quite significant number of people had begun to challenge the traditions, institutions and beliefs of the British establishment. These included social critics, and a group of artists and writers known as the Vorticists. They felt that Edwardian England had grown stale, corrupt and decadent, and that it needed to be shocked out of its complacency. When the war began, this way of thinking became more widespread. The war was therefore seen by some as a good thing: it offered an opportunity to shake things up, to make a fresh start, or to return to an earlier way of life that was more pure, healthy and vigorous.

Language, style and attitude

Activity

Read the extract from *War and Literature* by Edmund Gosse on page 24.
- What is Gosse's view of the war?
- Comment on the imagery he uses in lines 1–4.

Discussion

- Gosse clearly expresses the view that the war has been a huge shock to the system. He suggests that this was necessary and beneficial, and has brought *refreshment*, even if this is of a *solemn* nature (7). England has been in a state of *national decay* (18), its people living in an *opium-dream* (13), like drug addicts who have lost touch with reality. Life has been too easy, and they have become lazy and lethargic. The war has *awakened* them to *the strong red glare of reality* (24–25).
- The imagery in lines 1–4 is very powerful. A *scavenger* suggests a carrion bird or an animal picking the bones of corpses. War is destroying *thought*, but the old ways of thinking were already dead. *Condy's Fluid* was a strong disinfectant, and he suggests that the war's *red stream of blood* will have a similarly cleansing effect on people's minds, which have become like *stagnant pools*. These are rather gruesome metaphors, but they suggest that the war is somehow refreshing and invigorating.

Disillusionment

As the war literally became bogged down in stalemate, and was fought sometimes repeatedly over the same ground, it is not surprising that for men at the Front the war began to seem endless, and its meaning questionable. The traditional motives for fighting – patriotism and the belief in a just war supported by God – began to wear thin.

Activity

Read the extract from *Under Fire* by Henri Barbusse, which was written towards the end of 1915 (page 44).

Interpretations

What mood does Barbusse create here, and how does he use language to challenge traditional views about war?

Discussion

The mood of the extract is one of despair and hopelessness, along with a strange sense of disconnection or unreality. Although the injured men at the first-aid post are given vague identities, they don't seem to be real individuals, or entirely human. One is simply referred to as *some invisible creature* (44). The characters are more like representative figures who speak for all the men *stuck* in the war, *like the emblems of a varied collection of sufferings and miseries* (6–8). They are compared to survivors of a shipwreck, *clinging to this kind of boat* (6) and they also seem like souls in torment in hell, or limbo. The description of the setting, with *the half-light stagnating in the cellar* (1–2), adds to this effect.

The men have been damaged in all sorts of ways, mentally and physically, and they all utter cries of distress, but they seem somehow isolated from each other, caught up in their own pain. In particular, we are shown how the war has rapidly destroyed their youth. No longer *young and clean*, they have *filthy old* bodies (36, 37) and one is described as having a *rickety withered face* (40–41). The image of eager young heroes, like those in the early war poems, is well and truly shattered.

A key idea in the passage is the aviator's vision. His aerial overview of the war makes no more sense than the experience of the men on the ground, and threatens to drive him *insane* (97). From above, he sees that both sides say the same prayers and claim the support of the same God, shouting *identical yet contrary things* (104). The soldiers' discussion (from line 98) calls into question not only the righteousness of the war, but the nature and existence of God.

Activity

Look at the sonnet by Rupert Brooke on page 25, and then read the letter from Roland Leighton on page 31.

Compare the ways in which these two writers present the idea of dying for one's country.

Language, style and attitude

Discussion

Brooke presents a traditional, idealized view of death in war, which is very remote from reality. The poem is full of abstract concepts, such as *Holiness*, *Honour* and *Nobleness*, and these words are given capital letters, which adds to their impressiveness and makes the idea of death seem romantic, although rather vague. Dying for one's country is seen as a privilege; in the first line, the *Dead* are described as *rich*, and they are worshipped for the sacrifices they have made. They were ideal young men who, it seems, deliberately chose to give up their ideal lives of *work and joy* followed by a *serene* old age (6).

Leighton, writing from the Front, amid the wreckage of earlier battles, picks up Brooke's *stirring words of exhortation* (16–17) and uses them with bitter irony. He wants to confront those who write or believe such words with the reality of war, which is very different. His graphic descriptions of rotted corpses – the pitiful *little pile of sodden grey rags that cover half a skull and a shin bone* (20–21) and the *foetid heap of hideous putrescence* (27–28) – take him as far away as possible from the ideas contained in abstract words such as *Honour*,

Rupert Brooke in 1915

Glory, and *Valour* (14, 17). Like Brooke he capitalizes these words, but this only serves to emphasize his bitterness. He suggests the young men have not chosen to sacrifice their lives, but have done so *unknowing* (13), in pointless ignorance, for the sake of mere words rather than for anything tangible. These concepts and ideals are empty, he suggests, and invoking them is like praying to a non-existent or powerless heathen god (see Notes page 110).

Describing the indescribable

In a letter to his wife, the war artist Paul Nash (see also page 117) tells her that what he has seen at the Front is 'unspeakable, utterly indescribable' and that 'no pen or drawing can convey this country… only being in it and of it can ever make you sensible of its dreadful nature'. Writers often struggled with the sense that the war was full of such extreme experiences it was impossible to find words in which to communicate with those who had not shared them.

Because of the increasing mechanization of the war, in which killing was done at a distance and soldiers felt themselves becoming mere numbers, rather than individuals, there was a growing sense of depersonalization. Life in the trenches was so shocking that men became dehumanized and traumatized. Dissociation, the psychological mechanism by which we try to block out feelings and experiences that are too horrific or overwhelming to bear, was often the only way men could get through.

Near the end of his novel *Under Fire*, Henri Barbusse (see page 44) imagines a conversation between soldiers who are at the end of their tether and close to drowning in mud. One of them tries to describe his feeling that war is so 'unimaginable and immeasurable in time and space' that it 'stifles words'. What they have seen and been through is 'too much' for the human mind to hold: 'We're not built to take all this in. It buggers off in every direction: we're too small.' Yet they are determined to try to remember and speak out about their experience in order that

Language, style and attitude

there should be 'no more wars after this one' (Barbusse, pages 303–304).

Many writers similarly felt that it was important to make this attempt, in order to alert people to the true horror and consequences of war. Poets such as Siegfried Sassoon and Wilfred Owen, who were influenced by Barbusse, became convinced that the reality of war could be a suitable subject for poetry, provided it was approached in a genuinely truthful and compassionate way.

However, as combatant writers attempted to describe the reality of their experience, they found that language was stretched to its limits. Formal language and traditional imagery were no longer adequate. Some writers attempted direct, graphic description, as Robert Graves does in *A Dead Boche* (page 32) and Sassoon does in *Counter-Attack* (page 52); Barbusse (and some later novelists, such as Frederic Manning) abandoned falsely polite language and tried to replicate the real ways men spoke to each other. Many writers explored the possibilities of metaphor, simile, sound effects such as alliteration, and other more unusual techniques.

Activity
Look at the letter by Wilfred Owen on page 48. How does he try to convey the 'indescribable' nature of the war?

Discussion
When Owen attempts to describe No Man's Land, he uses the most extreme ideas and images he can think of, but also suggests that these are nowhere near strong enough to convey the reality. He likens it to the *Slough of Despond*, which in John Bunyan's allegorical *Pilgrim's Progress* is the place of utmost despair, yet, he says, this *could be contained in one of its crater-holes* (41–42). Sodom and Gomorrah (see Notes page 117) are the most evil, corrupt places he can think of, but they *could not light a candle* to the hideousness of No Man's Land (42–43).

Interpretations

Activity

Look at the extract from the historian R.H. Tawney's account of his experience of the battle of the Somme (page 36).

Read lines 34–76 closely. Make notes on how Tawney uses language and imagery here to try to convey what the bombardment was like.

Discussion

Here are some of the points you may have noted.

- The senses of sight and hearing are linked, and the boundary between them is blurred as the intensity of the sound seems to grow and merge with the *brilliance* (37) of the summer morning. He returns to this idea, describing sound in visual terms, when he tries to capture the way the appalling noise seems to hang in the air, indefinitely, as *a stationary panorama of sound* (51–52).
- Powerful words such as *bewildering tumult* (36) suggest that the sound is overwhelming to the mind and senses. He tells us he is attempting to describe sounds that are far beyond any previous experience, in both *magnitude* and *quality* (39, 40); the sound is *supernatural* (49).
- He cannot describe this sound in ordinary terms, as a *noise*, but resorts to metaphor: *it was a symphony* (43). All the different explosive sounds combine like the musical instruments of an orchestra to make one overall, continuous effect.
- The sound fills the air, which he personifies as *writhing* and a *tormented element* (54). The air becomes a being that suffers *a vast and agonised passion* (44–45) and makes every sound that expresses pain: it *groans*, *sighs*, and utters *shrill screams and pitiful whimpers* (45–46).
- The vibration is so powerful that he imagines his hand would be torn off, if he lifted it into the air, by *a whirlpool revolving with cruel and incredible velocity* (56–57).
- His description of the emotional effect is interesting. Not only does the noise fill him with *awe*, but he is also swept along by a kind of mad excitement or exhilaration – *exultation* – at the sheer power of it all (58, 59).

Although *In Parenthesis*, by David Jones, was written some years after the war, it is based on his own experiences as a private in the

Language, style and attitude

Royal Welsh Fusiliers. This long prose-poem is a piece of modernist writing, in which language is used in experimental and innovative ways. Jones writes in a way that is both dense and delicate, mixing highly poetic language with down-to-earth, vernacular expression. His many references to Welsh history and mythology, as well as all kinds of other texts, make *In Parenthesis* quite demanding to read, but very rich.

Activity

Read the extract from *In Parenthesis* (page 41) in which David Jones describes the experience of being on night manoeuvres. It is worth reading this text closely and looking at the notes that Jones provided for the text, which are included on pages 113–114.

How does he make his evocation interesting and effective?

Discussion

Jones takes the reader right into the midst of his experience, so that we almost have the sense of being one of the men finding their way through the dark landscape. It has the effect of an interior monologue, or stream of consciousness. Although he sometimes uses a third-person perspective, Jones records each detail as it comes into his mind, following trains of thought and associations of ideas. For example, the moonlight brings to mind a prayer – *shine on us* – and then the words of an old lullaby, *I want you* [the moon] *to play with/ and the stars as well* (41–43).

Jones's descriptions are highly evocative, which sometimes gives a very beautiful effect, even when he is describing damaged trees and military telephone wires. Under the moonlight, these become *a silver scar with drenched tree-wound; silver-trace a festooned slack; faery-bright a filigree* (37–38). Notice the delicate alliteration on 'f' and 's', which adds to the moon's softening effect. The explosion of a shell reflected in puddles produces *light orange flame-tongues in the long jagged water-mirrors where their feet go* (70–71).

This type of description is juxtaposed with the colloquial language of the men's dialogue, which is plain and down to earth (such as the repeated *Mind the hole*), their curses (*Left be buggered*, 60) and their dialect (*Sorry mate – you all right china?*, 61). Some of the men are Welsh, others are East London Cockney (see Notes pages 113–114).

149

Interpretations

When the men come upon a huge shell crater, we are given a real physical sense of the way they feel it, even though they are unable to see it: *they felt its vacuous pitness in their legs* (26–27).

We may also detect an ironic, dry, resigned humour in some of the narrator's comments, for example *and do we trapse dementedly round phantom mulberry bush* (22–23) – where we can also hear the Welsh intonation of the writer's voice (the inversion *do we* is typical in Welsh dialect).

Jones also uses an effective extended metaphor in which the whole scene is compared to a puppet show or mime act on stage. By moonlight, the men and their shadows look like *marionettes* (76) or *fantastic troll-steppers* (79) under floodlights, until clouds cover the moon and darkness falls like the *drop* curtain in the theatre.

Close-ups and distance shots

If you consider the texts in the section 'Under Fire' (pages 33–57), you may notice two contrasting ways of approaching the subject. One is to look at the war on the large scale, as a vast impersonal force. This involves being outside and probably at a distance, as an observer, seeing the whole picture. In several texts, writers or characters describe witnessing the war from a vantage point above the level of the battlefield. From there, they present aerial views that are like 'distance shots' of the war. At other times, the writer or character is firmly on the ground, in the trenches, or in the thick of battle. The focus is on the experience of individuals and their thoughts and feelings. This viewpoint shows the war in close-up and is much more personal.

Activity

Look at the extract from Rudyard Kipling's *France at War* on page 33, and the poem *Counter-Attack* by Siegfried Sassoon on page 52.
- In each text, what is the viewpoint? Where are the writer and the reader positioned in relation to the war?
- What is the effect of this in each case?

Language, style and attitude

Discussion

In the extract by Kipling, he writes in the first person, but as an outsider. His position is that of a reporter, describing the war for an audience of readers back in England. He is taken by a French officer to an observation post in a tall tree, a vantage point above and at a distance from the front line. From there he presents an aerial view of the conflict, using imagery of the sea to describe the distant gunfire and exploding shells, which become *the high-flung heads of breakers spouting white up the face of a groyne* (51–52). The effect is to make the war look *as impersonal as the drive of the sea along a breakwater* (48–49).

Although Kipling refers to the war as *the Devil and all his works* (37) and describes the *chemical yellow* of the landscape as *foul* (82), the impact of the war is blurred and the horror seems diminished when seen from such a distance.

Sassoon's poem, on the other hand, is very much a close-up view of the war. The poet narrates an incident in the first person, although he remains one of a group and does not refer directly to himself or make his own thoughts and feelings explicit. In the first stanza, he takes us with him into a trench, full of the dead, who are described in utterly repulsive, personal detail. Their *naked sodden buttocks, mats of hair* and *Bulged, clotted heads* (11–12) draw a visceral response from the reader.

The viewpoint then shifts slightly in the second stanza as he focuses in on one individual soldier. Although this man is referred to in the third person as *he*, the remainder of the poem is experienced from his point of view. Along with the poet, the reader seems to be down on the ground, in the midst of the horror, and sharing in this man's reluctance and *galloping fear* (22), the haste and clumsy turmoil of the attack and counter-attack, and finally his death. The poem is full of physical description: the bodily experience of being embroiled in the war is powerfully evoked.

Activity

Now look at Wilfred Owen's poem *The Show* on page 55.
- Consider the viewpoint of this poem and its effect.
- Compare this with the two texts in the previous activity.

Interpretations

Discussion

The Show gives a long-distance, aerial view of the battlefield. It is a first-person account, but not a factual one. The poet describes a dream or fantasy of an out-of-body experience – perhaps the result of shell shock – in which, accompanied by the personification of Death, he looks down on the sinister, sick landscape, in which he can see the lines of soldiers on both sides. From above, they do not look like a collection of individuals, but like writhing or *shrivelled* (9) caterpillars of brown and grey, *dithering* (16) among the *slimy paths* (10) of the trenches.

Unlike Kipling's report, where the horror of war is partly defused by being described from a distance, Owen's poem is powerful and shocking. Although we are distanced from the battlefield, the imagery of disease, with vocabulary such as *sweats* (3) and *pocks and scabs* (5), and of the strange cannibalistic creatures that attack and devour each other, evokes feelings of dread and repulsion. Sassoon's close-up view in *Counter-Attack* is gruesome and hard-hitting and communicates bodily experiences of shock and disgust. However, Owen's aerial image of the opposing armies is horrifying too. Perhaps because we know that these *caterpillars* are in fact made up of multitudes of individual men suffering *agonies* (22), the distancing and depersonalization are all the more appalling.

Wilfred Owen in 1916

Conflicts and contrasts

The literature of the First World War is full of contrasts. It has been suggested that the oppositional nature of war leads to a tendency to see things in 'black and white', in terms of two-sided splits or dichotomies, which Paul Fussell calls 'the versus habit' (*The Great War and Modern Memory*, page 79). To start with, there is the inevitable separation of allies and enemies, 'us' and 'them'.

Them and us

Although few would have disputed that the basic premise of the war was to try to win it, the ways in which the 'enemy' was experienced and presented varies considerably, depending on the viewpoint of the writer or character.

On the national scale, in propaganda, the war was presented as a battle between the forces of good and evil. Soldiers in the trenches sometimes viewed things rather differently. For example, Barbusse, in *Under Fire*, suggests that soldiers of both sides and all nations have more in common with each other than they do with those at home or those controlling the war. They are all victims of a vast, impersonal force that seems to have little meaning, and war itself is the only thing that should be fought against. 'Two armies fighting is like one great army killing itself,' he writes (page 306).

Activity

Look at the final section of the extract by Rudyard Kipling (pages 35–36) and read the extract from Florence L. Barclay's story, *My Heart's Right There* (page 69).

What attitudes to the war and the enemy do we find in the words of the French officer and of Polly's husband, Jim?

Discussion

The French officer, in Kipling's extract, sums up the war as a battle of *civilization* against the uncivilized *barbarian* (99–102). The enemy is

Interpretations

not individualized and not even referred to as 'the Germans'. They are *those brutes yonder*, which makes them sound like animals rather than people. The front line of battle is *the frontier of civilization*, which keeps these evil, less-than-human creatures at bay.

In Florence L. Barclay's story, Jim makes this even more explicit. He says *We ain't only fighting against **men**, out there. We're fighting the Devil* (36–37). He goes on to suggest that God is on the side of the Allies and that the war is *more than a fight for earthly crowns and kingdoms* but is a battle *for right and justice, against treachery and wrong* (57–61). He believes firmly that the war is *a righteous war* (62) against the forces of evil. He speaks with the voice of an individual who has wholeheartedly accepted nationalistic, patriotic propaganda, and uses all its traditional terms.

Activity

Now look at the account of Christmas 1914 by Frederick Chandler (page 29) and the poem *To Germany* by Charles Hamilton Sorley (page 30). How do these writers view the 'enemy'?

Discussion

In describing how he and his comrades give a German a decent burial, Chandler suggests that it was a point of honour for a *true British soldier* (7–8) to respect the German dead as well as their own.

Both Chandler and Sorley believe that ordinary soldiers on both sides are not responsible for the war. They *do not understand* what the war is about (Sorley, line 4) and *there is not a combatant soldier in any of the combatant armies who would not make peace tomorrow* (Chandler, lines 11–13).

Chandler says he had *no feeling of hatred in* [his] *heart at this time* (19–20), although later he was apparently less forgiving. Sorley says the warring soldiers must *hiss and hate* now, but looks forward to when they are no longer *blind* but able to see properly *each other's truer form* (8–10).

Each writer empathizes with the 'enemy' and sees that he is a human being like himself. Chandler imagines how the dead German might have celebrated Christmas *in the warmth of the home* he loves (14); Sorley recognizes that German soldiers saw their *future bigly planned* (5) just as he did.

Chandler goes on to describe the *amazing* (25) truce of Christmas 1914, when 'enemies' fraternized and *all was good fellowship and a pathetic friendliness* (36). The word *pathetic* suggests a kind of desperation in the way they reach out to each other as well as the sad recognition that such *friendliness* is doomed.

The tendency to split and polarize – to see things in terms of opposites – can be seen in many other aspects of the war and is clearly reflected in the literature. Divisions arose, for example, between men who joined the army and civilians who did not, and between men and women who were unable to communicate about the experiences they had not shared. Other contrasts are also striking. There was the difference between the grim life in the trenches and the comforts of home. The smart restaurants and theatres of London were often less than 100 miles away but might have been on another planet. Many writers also recorded the stark, ironic juxtaposition of the beauty and power of nature against the ugliness and devastation of the war-torn landscape.

German soldiers lie dead on the Somme battlefield

Interpretations

Combatants and non-combatants

Those who were directly involved in the conflict – the ordinary soldiers or privates, and the junior and mid-ranking officers who fought alongside them – became known as 'combatants'. Others – women, civilian men (such as those who were too old to fight, incapacitated in some way, or in 'reserved' jobs), and non-fighting army staff – were 'non-combatants'.

At home, propaganda presented the war in optimistic terms and idealistic language. For example, on 3 July 1916 *The Times* reported of the first day of the Battle of the Somme that 'everything has gone well… we got our first thrust well home and there is every reason to be most sanguine as to the result'. It is not surprising that most civilians had little idea of what it was like for men at the Front.

Meanwhile, as the troops experienced heavy casualties and increasing horrors, the gulf between combatants and non-combatants widened. Siegfried Sassoon wrote bitterly about this lack of understanding in poems such as *Blighters*, in which he imagines a tank mowing down the cackling audience in a music hall, and *The Glory of Women*, where he contrasts women's ideas about the 'heroism' of soldiers with the realities of the battlefield.

Although non-combatants could not comprehend the full horror of trench warfare, in some parts of England the reality was brought home more forcibly by the first air raids, which were launched from Zeppelin airships. In his novel *Mr Britling Sees It Through*, H.G. Wells explores how the attitude of one ordinary non-combatant could be changed through less direct experiences of the war. Mr Britling, a typical 'little Briton', is initially keen to contribute to the war effort, but is too old for military service. Gradually the war impinges more and more on the lives of his comfortable, middle-class circle. By the time his own beloved son has been killed and he hears that a young German friend has also died in the war, he has come to question the whole meaning of the war. The extract on page 76 is from the middle of the novel: an elderly relative of Mr Britling has just died after a Zeppelin attack.

Conflicts and contrasts

Activity

Read the extract from *Mr Britling Sees It Through* (page 76).
- How is Mr Britling's attitude altered by this experience?
- Comment on the tone in which he refers to the German air raid.

Discussion

Mr Britling realizes that up to this point his knowledge of the war has been merely general, and based on fantasy, or false *representations* (64). Now, however, the reality of war has been brought home to him with a *raw and quivering focus* (69). Through recognizing the individual suffering of his cousin, he comes to realize that this is only a *sample* (74) of the *agony* (71) shared by millions of victims of the war, each of whom is likewise an individual *worthy of respect and care* (73). He sees the *dense cruel stupidity* of war, *plain and close* (60–61).

Wells sarcastically refers to the German action in bombing the town as *brilliant* (23). He vividly describes the horrific details of the raid and its consequences, including the screaming of the *mutilated child* (13) and Aunt Wilshire's *bleeding wounds and shattered bones* (52), but points out that the number of casualties is relatively small and that most of them were women and children. It is hardly a significant victory for the Germans, but he bitterly imagines them nevertheless *buzzing* home (54) in triumph to medals and a heroes' welcome. He compares their supposed enjoyment of meaningless destruction to that of boys who have thrown a stone through a window and run away.

Officers and men

Not only did the troops feel estranged from civilians at home, but there was also a split between them and the staff officers of the army. Higher ranking officers and those with administrative roles, who stayed well behind the lines and out of danger, were often despised or resented by the fighting men.

Interpretations

Activity

Read the extract from *Parade's End* by Ford Madox Ford (page 87).
- How does Ford present the character of the staff officer, Colonel Levin?
- What can you detect about Captain Tietjens' attitude towards Levin, and Sergeant-Major Cowley's attitude to both of them?

Discussion

Levin is described as *gentlemanly* (2) and his fancy uniform immediately makes him stand out. The *strikingly scarlet hat-band* was only worn by those in safe positions – it would be highly visible and therefore impractical in the firing line. He is *cheerful* (14) and relaxed, as if he has *a century of the battalion headquarters' time to waste* (17–18). He also has time to be vain about his appearance. He admires his own *perfectly elegant knees* (58) and brushes them with a handkerchief. He is totally out of touch with Tietjens and his men, who have just witnessed a death and are working under pressure. Ford indicates he has an upper-class accent: he has a *slight lisp* (15) and addresses Cowley as *sergeant-majah*.

Levin sounds rather effeminate and ineffectual when he exclaims *Dear, dear! Dear, dear!* (25) and Ford effectively describes his rather precise, fastidious way of speaking when we are told he *used the word hell as if he had first wrapped it in eau-de-Cologned cotton-wadding* (26–28). He seems unused to being anywhere near the violence of war, as he jumps away in horror when he realizes he is standing on the spot where a soldier has died only a short time before. He appears more concerned about getting blood on his *beautiful, shining, knee-high aircraft boots* (82) than about the casualty. He also comes across as a snob, dismissing the dead soldier as *Only a Glamorganshire* (97–98).

Although the narrative is in the third person, the viewpoint is usually that of Tietjens. Tietjens speaks to the colonel politely and calls him *sir*, but it is obvious that he regards him with contempt. He recognizes the colonel from civilian life and knows that he has gained a good safe staff job in the army not because he is intelligent or talented, but because of his family connections. We can tell that Tietjens is dismissive and unimpressed when he thinks of the

Conflicts and contrasts

colonel as *G.S.O.II, or something* (5), as a *staffwallah* (15) or *this fellow* (29), and refers to his fancy epaulettes as *cavalry gadgets* (32).

The sergeant-major is an N.C.O. – a non-commissioned officer. This means that he has been promoted from the ranks of the ordinary soldiers as a result of being good at his job, not because he is of a higher social class. Although Tietjens is his commanding officer, Ford suggests that Cowley is really the one who manages the situation. He knows how to handle the staff officer, putting on a performance and being obsequiously polite, like a shop assistant in an up-market store, yet at the same time undermining him. The way he speaks gives the impression that he *might as well have said 'madam' as 'sir'* (48). Cowley is very loyal to Tietjens, but evidently sees him as being in need of looking after, as he tries to defend him from the colonel, *as you protect your infant daughters in lambswool from draughts* (13–14).

The view that those in command were out of touch with reality and indifferent to the suffering of their men became widespread, and it features in several poems by Siegfried Sassoon and Wilfred Owen. (See, for example, *The Parable of the Old Man and the Young*, in the Oxford Student Texts edition of *Wilfred Owen: Selected Poems and Letters*.) Poor strategy and lack of planning are said to have cost many lives during the Battle of the Somme, among others. The phrase 'lions led by donkeys' is often used to describe the idea that brave soldiers were sacrificed by stubborn, incompetent old generals, and it has become part of the mythology of the First World War. This view was popularized in the 1960s, and it is clearly represented in the extract from the satirical show *Oh What a Lovely War* on page 90. However, more recent historical commentators suggest that this way of thinking may be an over-simplification.

Activity

In a small group, read through the extract from *Oh What a Lovely War*. Discuss or experiment with different ways of presenting the

Interpretations

scene, which takes place when the characters are on 'Sunday parade', an open-air church service.
- Make notes on some of the ways satire is used effectively in the extract.
- Comment on the portrayal of Sir Douglas Haig.

Discussion
Here are some points you may have noted.
- In this satirical version of a church service, each character is involved in a 'private' conversation with God and is apparently oblivious to the others and to the hymn-singing soldiers, whereas the audience is aware of the ironic interplay between their different voices.
- The Chaplain is naïve and superstitious; he prays for Sir Douglas Haig, not for the men who will be endangered in *tomorrow's onset* (4–5), and follows this with a series of unfortunately chosen, clichéd lines from hymns and prayers. Soldiers in the trenches probably will not be very *cleanly* (38), for example; neither are they likely to *depart* (die) *in peace* (15–16). The Nurse seems at first to have a more realistic view, expecting *enormous numbers of dead and wounded* (41–42), but then contradicts this with a childlike certainty that God will answer her prayer.
- It is clearly suggested here that Haig is complacent, vain and too self-important to accept orders from a *junior foreign commander* (34). He gives away the fact that he wants to claim victory for himself *before the Americans arrive* (39–40), which makes him sound rather childish or jealous. He does not mention the ordinary soldiers who will have to do the fighting, and is only concerned with his own prestige.

War and nature

Nature features frequently in First World War literature. The Georgian movement in poetry, which influenced many poets of the war generation, was concerned with the English landscape and rural ways of life. Writers were attuned to noticing nature

Conflicts and contrasts

and their surroundings, even in the midst of war.

However, what was often most striking was the way the beauty of nature highlighted or contradicted the ugliness and devastation of a landscape blighted by war. This gave rise to many incongruous juxtapositions. For example, R.H. Tawney draws attention to the *glorious* summer weather and the *intenser blue of the July sky* (34, 38), which formed the ironic counterpoint to the slaughter of the first days of the Battle of the Somme (see page 37). Siegfried Sassoon adds larks and glowing poppies to the scene, which he calls 'a sunlit picture of hell' in his semi-fictional *Memoirs of an Infantry Officer*. Other writers describe fabulous dawns and sunsets over a battlefield strewn with corpses, or reflected in water-filled shell craters.

Devastated trees on a battlefield at the Western Front in 1917

Interpretations

Activity

Read the letter by Paul Nash on page 50.

How does Nash effectively describe the interplay between war and nature here?

Discussion

Nash sees everything around him with the eyes of an artist who is used to finding inspiration from the natural world. This distances him slightly, as he sees even what has been destroyed in terms of interesting shapes and artistic images. He is *excited* by the *wonderful ruinous forms* and *toast-rackety roofs* of a bombed village (50–52). He notices small details and identifies flowers and plants. In particular, he has a precise awareness of colour and light, from the *green and warm lovely lights* (7) of returning spring and the *bright gold* of dandelions (16) to the way *brilliant growths of bright green* stand out against the *pinky colour* of the dried mud (46, 42).

Although he mainly responds to the visual, other senses play a part too. He notices the *intoxicating smell* of violets (10–11) and the *moist perfume* of new vegetation (69) as well as the way *the birds sing... in spite of shells and shrapnel* (48–49).

Nash also relates the war to the climate, suggesting it has come to seem just as eternal and inexorable as the changing of the seasons. In the same way that people find ways to deal with bad weather, they will become inured to the war: *we shall get used to it just as we are almost accustomed to the damnable climate of England* (35–37).

Most importantly, he is struck by the *Ridiculous mad incongruity!* (25) of the way nature continues to flourish even in places that the war has rendered *desolate* and *ruinous* (20, 21). Even *the most broken trees* (22), growing in soil poisoned by gas, have sprouted new leaves. He describes a shattered wood as having a *bruised heart* from which he hears *the throbbing song of a nightingale* (24–25). The words *heart* and *throbbing* have an emotional resonance, suggesting that the wood has suffered, but lives on. Like war, nature seems *absurd* (26) in this context. Despite the war, spring still comes round, like a rebirth, with its lush vegetation; *Flowers bloom everywhere* and *the place is just joyous* (13–16). Nature's power to regenerate seems even stronger than war's power to destroy.

Conflicts and contrasts

Nash admits that being in the trenches gives life a *new zest* and *greater meaning* (58, 57). Above all, it heightens his sense of *the significance of nature*, which is *full of surprises* (59, 60). The beauty of the world seems sharper and *more poignant* (58) when juxtaposed with a deformed landscape and the threat of annihilation.

Nature is not always a benevolent force, however. Although its beauty could bring some comfort to men in the trenches, it could also be deadly. The weather sometimes posed as much of a threat as the enemy. Lives were lost to the cold and rain, while frostbite, trench foot – an infection caused by having cold, wet feet for too long – and other diseases caused great suffering. Some men literally froze to death in wintry conditions, and others drowned in the worst of the mud.

Writers such as Henri Barbusse and Wilfred Owen effectively portray the more hostile aspects of nature. In Owen's poem *Exposure*, men wait indefinitely in freezing conditions for action to start, *But nothing happens*.

Activity

Read *Exposure* by Wilfred Owen (page 54). Discuss or make notes on the ways in which Owen presents the forces of nature.

Discussion

The bitterly cold wind is lethal – it *knives* the soldiers (1). The alliteration of 's' sounds in *merciless iced east winds* mimics the winds' sinister hiss. Their *mad gusts* are described, disturbingly, as being like the death throes of dying men caught in the barbed wire (6–7). The word *nonchalance* (19) suggests the wind has a casual attitude, not caring what harm it causes.

As dawn approaches, the wind brings with it *ranks on shivering ranks of grey* (14). These are heavy snow clouds, but become identified with the 'ranks' of the enemy, as German soldiers wore grey. However, the *Attacks* from the clouds are just as threatening, and equally dangerous.

Interpretations

As snow fills the air, blown *sidelong* by the wind (18), it is more deadly than *flights of bullets* (16). The alliteration in *flowing flakes that flock* maintains the sinister effect, suggesting the snowflakes are soft but suffocating.

In stanza 5, as the men begin to succumb to exposure, the soldiers become drowsy and dream of *grassier ditches* at home, with *blossoms* and *blackbird*, where they doze in the sun. However, these pleasant natural images are dangerous too. If the men follow them too far and fall asleep in the snow, they risk hypothermia and freezing to death.

In the final stanza, we are confronted with the horrific vision of men freezing as the mud turns to ice. The frost *will fasten* on them, suggesting a monster gripping them between its jaws until they are shrivelled and *crisp*. We are left with the terrifying image of the frozen eyes of *All* – both living and dead.

Heroes and cowards

One complex question raised by the war was what it really means to be a hero.

Activity

Read the extract from *A Subaltern on the Somme*, by Max Plowman (page 26).

What are Plowman's thoughts and feelings as he sets off for the Front? Discuss whether you think he is brave and heroic.

Discussion

Plowman describes very mixed feelings. He refers to the waiting trains as *snakes* (14), which gives them a sinister air and hints at his underlying fear. He also suggests they have become powerful *masters* and *instruments of destiny* (15, 17), which now have control over his life. His impulse is to escape and get as far away as possible – to *drive till the car breaks down* (30).

He says he is *hideously self-conscious* (18) and far too aware of his appearance. He seems to take some pride in looking like a *voluntary* hero, but he only *faintly* feels the pleasure of flattery (20–21). He finds some comfort in the *reality* of the love he shares with his wife, beside which *Nothing else matters* (46, 47), and also in the knowledge that they have a child, *Love's embodiment*, which is one way in which he can live on and achieve *victory over death* (49–53).

However, most of his energy goes into suppressing the *violence and revolt* of his mind, which he compares in a simile to *a cloud brooding above my body* (22–23). This effectively captures the feeling of his struggle to hide his fear, to stay in control of himself and behave in the cool, undemonstrative ways that are expected. He certainly is not fearless, but he manages to keep a 'stiff upper lip' and the appearance of bravery.

We have seen that early in the war, the ideal of heroism was expressed in archaic, abstract terms. Look, for example at the propaganda recruiting poem by the Bishop of Exeter, *Give Us Men* (page 25), which calls for:

> Men of lofty aim and action...
> Men who, when the tempest gathers,
> Grasp the Standard of their fathers
>   In the thickest fight:
> Men who strike for home and altar,
> (Let the coward cringe and falter,)
>
> (lines 9, 13–17)

This stereotypical hero is also expected to be *free and frank* (3), *loyal* (6), and *Tender* as well as *brave* (20). He is clearly distinguished from the cringing coward.

However, once men are embroiled in the reality of the *thickest fight*, the distinction between 'hero' and 'coward' often seems much less clear, particularly when viewed with hindsight.

Activity

Look again at R.H. Tawney's account of what it was like to participate in the Battle of the Somme (page 36). How does he describe his experience, and what does he suggest about heroism in battle?

Interpretations

Discussion

We noted earlier (page 148) that while he was preparing for battle, the sound of the massive bombardment had filled Tawney with a *triumphant exultation* (59).

He admits he had been worried about going 'over the top', fearing he might lose his nerve and fail to live up to expectations at the last minute – that he might *crack* and be found *rotten* (84–85). His worst fear was that he might put others' lives at risk. However, once he had taken the plunge, he tells us, *I felt a load fall from me* (77–78). He was released from all fear, became *happy and self-possessed* (90–91) and joyfully certain that he couldn't fail.

Reflecting on this, he says plainly that *It wasn't courage* (91). In his view, true bravery means being able to go ahead despite feeling fear and in full awareness of the risk of death. His experience was different. He felt dissociated – out of touch with reality – and went forward in an altered state in which he seemed to know *positively* that he could not be hurt (95). Some of his descriptions reflect the quality of dissociation; for example, when he describes three men lying in a shell hole looking *like fish in a basket* (126) he displays no emotional response.

On seeing the enemy, he does experience the desire to kill, but says it was as if he were taken over by the *beast* within himself (131). He is very honest about his state of mind and admits that he enjoyed shooting at the Germans, but he describes it as *insane* (141). He uses phrases such as *paleolithic savage* and *merry, mischievous ape* (130, 148), which suggest he had entered a state where he was no longer a civilized human being; killing had become a frivolous game.

Tawney is very clear that this kind of 'heroism' has little to do with real courage. What the newspapers ironically reported as the *sporting spirit* of the troops (150) was really men being carried away by a form of madness. Afterwards, he feels shame.

Activity

How does Sassoon present the soldiers in his sonnet *Dreamers* (page 53)? Are they heroic?

Conflicts and contrasts

Discussion

In this poem Sassoon considers soldiers from different perspectives, shifting from philosophizing about their role, to the reality of their life in the trenches, and then to what is going on in their minds. In the octet, *death's grey land* sounds vague and timeless. The soldiers are investing their lives in a future in which they may have no part.

Some of Sassoon's language here echoes traditional 'heroic' war poetry: *In the great hour of destiny they stand*, and they *are sworn to action* (3, 5). The idea that they are 'dreamers' may seem to hint that they have fantasies of becoming heroes. However, he goes on to make it clear that these are ordinary men of flesh and blood; *when the guns begin*, they dream not of heroic deeds, but of their *homes* and their *wives* (7–8).

In the sestet, after placing them in the grim reality of the *foul dugouts* and *ruined trenches*, Sassoon reveals their *hopeless longing* for the ordinary things they have left behind – and which they probably did not appreciate until now – even *going to the office in the train*.

If they are heroes, they are reluctant ones. Perhaps their heroism lies simply in their endurance.

It is of course easier to analyse the realities of 'heroism' in war from a distance. Looking back after many decades at the First World War, writers such as Susan Hill can consider the issue from a psychological point of view.

Activity

Read the extract from Susan Hill's *Strange Meeting* (page 93). What points are made about heroism here?

Discussion

Hilliard, describing his C.O., realizes that for a man to be *brave* he does not necessarily have to fit the stereotype of a hero. Garrett is *not an imaginative man. But careful, a good planner, cool headed* (26–27). This may be an equally valid manifestation of courage. However, when Garrett describes the chaotic action in which most of

Interpretations

his battalion died, very little about it seems 'heroic'. His men seem to have lost their heads, everyone *went mad*, and they *might have been a pack of schoolboys in a scrum* (77–78).

Many men, particularly those who were sensitive and thoughtful, or who were less able to shut down their feelings and block out what was most horrific, suffered greatly or became overwhelmed by their experiences in the trenches. Shell shock or neurasthenia – what we would today call post-traumatic stress disorder – with its symptoms of shaking, stammering, flashbacks and nightmares, even partial paralysis, was common. Some soldiers, naturally enough, found themselves simply unable to tolerate any more. Such 'faint-heartedness' was often dismissed as shirking and was heavily frowned upon and punished. Quite a few men were shot by their own colleagues, for 'cowardice'.

Activity
With a partner, read the extract from *Journey's End* by R.C. Sherriff (page 61). Discuss where your sympathies lie in this situation.

Discussion
You may have raised some of the following questions.
- Hibbert complains of neuralgia, which is almost impossible to diagnose, and is due to take part in an attack in a couple of days' time. Do you believe him, or do you think he is pretending? How much difference does this make? He sounds desperate; can you sympathize with his fear? If it is true that men can leave when they are sick but officers can't, is this fair? Do you respect Hibbert? Do you like him?
- Stanhope is responsible for his men and for their performance. Do you think he has a choice here? Is he fair or harsh in his treatment of Hibbert? Is he right to suggest Hibbert is a *shirker* (50)? He says: *Better die of the pain than be shot for deserting* (44–45). If it is true that Hibbert will be shot if he leaves the trench, is Stanhope acting in Hibbert's best interests? Why do you think he tells Hibbert that he too suffers from neuralgia? Do you believe him? Do you respect him? Do you like him?

Conflicts and contrasts

- By the end of the play, Hibbert has overcome his 'cowardice' and is ready to take part in the attack. How realistic is this, do you think?

You may find it interesting to compare the dialogue in *Journey's End* with the conversation between soldiers about to go over the top in the Battle of the Somme in the extract from *Observe the Sons of Ulster Marching Towards the Somme* by Frank McGuinness (page 97).

Some men who found life in the trenches beyond endurance resorted to self-inflicted wounds or even suicide. A wound that incapacitated the soldier but was not life-threatening was known among British soldiers as a 'blighty', and was seen as desirable because it offered an honourable way of being sent home. Perhaps it is not surprising that some desperate men were driven to injure themselves.

Rose Macaulay's anti-war novel *Non-Combatants and Others*, published in 1916, includes one of the first literary accounts of a self-inflicted wound.

Activity

Read the extract from *Non-Combatants and Others* (page 58). How does Rose Macaulay reveal the mental suffering of the soldiers through:
- Ingram's explanation
- how she presents Ingram's character
- what we learn about Alix's brother Paul?

Discussion

- Ingram explains that *nerves* can afflict all kinds of men. Even those you would least expect to break down – *chaps as cheery as crickets* who can endure a great deal while *never turning a hair* – can suddenly *go to pot* (16–23). But he also maintains that some men are more susceptible because they are *not strong enough in body or mind* and should not be in the trenches at all (28–29).

Interpretations

- Ingram himself reveals the effects of *nerves* through his own behaviour; he seems to be talking compulsively while putting on a brave face. Alix notices that although he looks *jolly*, he talks too fast and his *inward-looking eyes* suggest he is reliving events as he speaks (25–26). He is also likened to the *Ancient Mariner* (50), who is compelled to tell and retell his terrible story to anyone who will listen, as if in an attempt to exorcise it from his mind (see also Notes page 123).
- We learn that Paul was very young, just out of school, *nervous, sensitive… and delicate* (32–33). It is evident that he was shocked and traumatized, particularly after seeing *his best friend cut to pieces by a bit of shell before his eyes* (37–38). He had become sick and started *exposing himself* to enemy fire, deliberately trying to get hit (40). Finally he staged an 'accidental' shooting that proved fatal. He was discovered and *shamed* in front of the other men (57).

It is not surprising that, set against the massive scale and heavyweight mechanized weaponry of the war, men had little sense of personal power, and heroic ideals became meaningless. Samuel Hynes, in *A War Imagined: The First World War and English Culture* (1990), suggests that by 1917, 'The war itself had come to seem the only source of energy in its world: guns roared, bullets flew, armies moved; but individual men could only suffer' (page 208).

In the later years of the war, soldiers are often presented as victims, or even martyrs. We find this in the poems of Siegfried Sassoon and Wilfred Owen, but the idea is most strongly expressed in a book by Georges Duhamel, a French doctor and writer, who served as a military surgeon on the Western Front. The war itself ceased to have any meaning for him, but in his *La Vie des Martyrs* (translated as *The New Book of Martyrs*) he makes it his duty to record the stories of some of his patients: 'It was written that you should suffer without purpose and without hope. But I will not let all your sufferings be lost in the abyss.'

Conflicts and contrasts

Helping a wounded man back across the trenches from the front line

Activity

Read the extract from *The New Book of Martyrs* on page 63.
- How does Duhamel present his patient Leglise?
- What do we learn about Duhamel's own character and attitude to life?
- Why and how does he try to influence Leglise's decision?

Discussion

- Leglise faces a terrible choice between death and a life of helpless disability. Duhamel observes his patient carefully. He notices the signs of grief and despair. Leglise looks around *languidly* and *hardly seems to have made up his mind to live* (8–9). He suggests that Leglise feels tormented by the doctors who are frustrating his needs and wishes, in order to keep him alive: *he wants to die perhaps, and we will not let him* (14–15). He compares the young man's *bewildered* efforts to oppose the doctors to a man *rowing against the storm* (39–40). Despite his

Interpretations

situation, Leglise has dignity. He reiterates his desire to die with *mournful gravity* (61). Harrowingly, he also clutches at straws: he feels *joy* (78) at the slightest possibility that he might avoid the second amputation and still live. He tries to delay the decision – *Wait another day, please, please* (116–117) – as though there is still a spark of hope in him.

- Duhamel comes across as conscientious and compassionate. It is evident that he is deeply affected by his patient's predicament, possibly even too emotionally involved. He is able to enter imaginatively into his patient's experience (16–29). He is also a man with a sense of wonder and appreciation for life, nature and beauty. The knee is *a complicated, delicate marvel* (3–4) and he notices the beauty of the garden and the *warm star-decked night* (68); *in spite of war, the night is like waters dark and divine* (113–114).
- Despite his empathy for Leglise, Duhamel feels strongly that his desire to die is unnatural. It seems to him that nature cries out against Leglise's choice. Nature itself always chooses life: when he accidentally steps on a beetle, *it flies away in desperate haste* to save its own life (52) and he imagines the trees and insects all saying of Leglise *He is not right!* (50). He calls for nature's support in finding words that will convince Leglise that *it is sweet to live, even with a body so grievously mutilated* (73–74). He also promises Leglise that as he has sacrificed his legs for his country, France will not allow him to *suffer poverty and misery* (100). We can tell that Duhamel is very persuasive; he overrides the young man's *resistance* and *trivial objections* (93, 96). Do you think he was right to do so?

Activity

Now read the extract from *Now It Can Be Told*, by Philip Gibbs (page 85) and Wilfred Owen's poem *Disabled* (page 66).

According to these two writers, what future awaits soldiers who survive the war but are severely disabled?

Discussion

Gibbs asks: *Who cared for the men who... bore on their bodies the scars of war?* (49–50). He reports that in reality, disabled soldiers received very little support as they tried to rebuild their lives. They received meagre pensions or were *forgotten in institutions*. They were kept *hidden from the public eye*, perhaps because the sight of them would provoke discomfort or awkward questions (53–54).

In *Disabled*, Wilfred Owen foresees what this will mean in individual terms. A young soldier, severely disabled, waits helplessly in his wheelchair for nurses to put him to bed. Before he went to war he was lively and good-looking, and he enjoyed football and flirting with the girls. Now he sits in a *ghastly suit of grey/ Legless, sewn short at elbow* (2–3) and women look away from him in embarrassment, preferring *the strong men that were whole* (44). All that the future now holds for him is *a few sick years in institutes*, dependent on charity and *whatever pity they may dole* (40, 42).

Less than six months after the war, Gibbs suggests, *'our heroes', 'our brave boys in the trenches'* were left to fend for themselves (55). They received no special treatment or help from the nation they had served.

Men and women

In times of war, there has always been a tendency for gender differences to be more sharply defined. Men and women are assigned different roles: it is men's duty to fight for their country, to be chivalrous and to protect women and children, who are seen as vulnerable and dependent. Women, meanwhile, are expected to 'keep the home fires burning', to provide emotional support for their men and to have a civilizing influence. The conventional woman's role is a passive one. She is not valued for what she does herself; often all that is expected of her is the ability to wait patiently and to tolerate anxiety and grief. The poet Laurence Binyon sums it up in an early war poem entitled *To Women*:

> For you, you too to battle go,
> Not with the marching drums and cheers,
> But in the watch of solitude
> And through the boundless night of fears.

Interpretations

Activity

Read the extract from *My Heart's Right There*, by Florence L. Barclay (page 69). Discuss the characters of Jim and Polly. What do they suggest about what was expected of men and women in the war?

Discussion

Jim and Polly are stereotypically 'masculine' and 'feminine'. As Jim describes the dangers he has faced in the trenches, he slaps his thigh (1) and speaks *with eager interest* (27). He is the tough man of action, with a clear sense of his own role and the purpose of the war. He speaks firmly and with certainty: *'We're fighting the Devil... I'm telling you a solemn, awful truth'* (36–39).

Polly fulfils the conventional passive woman's role. She is the listener, not the participant. She speaks only twice, once to ask a question and once to echo the words Jim has told her women should say. Jim claims that he is not *a bit afraid to die* (21–22). Polly is the emotional one; she carries the fear for both of them and has *terror at her heart* (29), and her feelings show in her white face and trembling lips (84).

Jim illustrates the chivalrous ideal, saying – emotively – that men fight *to keep our homes safe, and our wives and little children free from perils worse than shot and shell* (58–60). Meanwhile, women are expected to be *brave* as well as men, but for a woman this means *letting her man go* and putting a brave face on her sacrifice (65–67). She must be a model of selfless loyalty: if he is killed, *she must stand up, brave and true – as a soldier's wife or a soldier's mother – and say: 'God save the King!'* (67–69).

However, not all women were happy to accept the traditional role. Cicely Hamilton, a suffragette, believed that for a nation to succeed in a war of this scale, *all* its citizens needed to be mobilized, and not just male combatants. In her poem *Non-Combatant* she expresses her frustration that women's abilities were being wasted. However, it was not long before women did become more actively involved. Although they never fought, many served as nurses or in auxiliary roles, while others worked in munitions factories or took the place of men in jobs that women had never done before.

Conflicts and contrasts

A young woman and an old man working at a munitions factory in Chilwell, Nottinghamshire in 1917

Activity

Read *Non-Combatant* (page 72). What is Cicely Hamilton so upset about?

Discussion

Hamilton feels bitterly rejected, because the *War-Lords* (4) are only interested in the work of men. She hates having to be *idle* and *cumbrous*: she feels like a *useless* burden to the country (5–6). She has talents and abilities and is desperately keen to contribute – *afire to give and give* – but *No man has need of me* (7, 9, 12).

Above all, her pride is hurt that she must accept *charity* (10). She is just another *mouth that must be fed* (15) and can do nothing in return. It causes her great suffering to *endure* this (17); it is like *a burning, beating wound* (13); but she decides that keeping a stiff upper lip and putting up with the situation is the only thing she can offer to the war effort.

Interpretations

Cicely Hamilton eventually found ways to use her talents through challenging war work, but not all women found this easy. May Sinclair was also desperate to be useful and managed to get to Belgium as a secretary and reporter with a field ambulance crew. She hoped to see some action and write *brilliant articles* about it (38) to raise money for the Field Ambulance Corps, but found herself up against all kinds of obstacles. Women were barred from anything except safe, trivial tasks.

Activity

Read the extract from *A Journal of Impressions in Belgium*, by May Sinclair (page 73).

May Sinclair is bored – but how does she make her account of the experience interesting and effective?

Discussion

Sinclair uses effective similes to describe the sinister presence of the airship (*Taube*) hovering above, comparing it to a hawk *watching its prey* (6).

She describes the dramatic ups and downs of her moods and emotions. She is so *weighed down by the sense of our uselessness* (20–21) that being allowed to undertake even small tasks makes her *foolishly elated* (19).

In lines 39–68, she uses an enormously long sentence to list all the situations where she might be able to help but is not allowed to, such as seeing *dripping stretchers, agonized bodies* and being *utterly powerless to help*. This rises in a crescendo as her suppressed anger builds, before she concludes *I can only say of the experience that I hope there is no depth of futility deeper than this to come*. She then bitterly jokes that it would be better to be a prisoner of the Germans because at least there would be *something to write about afterwards* (70–71). But ironically, she is finding plenty to say about her experience here. She adds, with bathos, *What's more, I'm bored*, which makes her seem very human.

Sinclair confides in the reader what she cannot tell the Commandant; she admits to an *insane ambition* (79–80), then tells us what it is not, before confessing that her true desire is to be in the thick of the action as a genuine ambulance worker, rather than a journalist. She wants to fulfil her *mad dream* and wear her *breeches like the men* (93–94).

Some of Sinclair's language is extreme; at times it would be equally appropriate to describe men's experience in the trenches. Forced inactivity is *the very refinement of hell* (95–96) and a *fatuous sacrifice of women's lives* (63–64).

Women's lives were affected by the war in many other ways. The loss of so many healthy young men resulted in a serious imbalance between the genders for the war generation. Large numbers of women lost their husbands or lovers; after the war, many were forced to remain single and embrace independent lifestyles that would have been unusual beforehand. Women who had taken on new roles during the war were reluctant to relinquish them, and in February 1918, women over 30 were finally granted the right to vote. Gender roles would never again be so clearly defined.

Activity

Look at these three texts:
- *Now It Can Be Told* by Philip Gibbs (page 85)
- Vera Brittain's response to the Armistice in *Testament of Youth* (page 82)
- Alan Bennett's *Waiting for the Telegram* (page 100).

What does each text reveal about the impact of the war on women's lives?

Discussion

- Gibbs suggests that many men and women struggled to rebuild their relationships after the war. Men could not communicate their experience, and women found that although they didn't look any different, *they had not come back the same men* (7–8). They had symptoms of post-traumatic stress disorder, which made them difficult to live with: they were *easily moved to passion when they lost control of themselves… bitter in their speech, violent in opinion, frightening* (11–13). Women, unable

Interpretations

>
> to comprehend, felt rejected: *'Are you tired of me?' said the young wife, wistfully* (21). Gibbs also mentions – rather dismissively – that *The girls were clinging to their jobs* (32) and did not want to relinquish their incomes. Women were now to some extent competing with men in the job market and *Employers favored girl labor, found it efficient and, on the whole, cheap* (34–35).

- Vera Brittain, who lost her brother, her fiancé and her friends, suggests that at the end of the war she is only one of many *to whom their best will never return* and who are left with *a heart that breaks* (27, 31). She is a *lonely survivor* (43), having lost *All those with whom I had really been intimate*, and now has no one with whom she can share *the heights and the depths* of her memories (84–86). She looks into the future with a sense of emptiness as she realizes that *everything that had hitherto made up my life had vanished with Edward and Roland, with Victor and Geoffrey* (91–93).
- In Violet's monologue in *Talking Heads*, Alan Bennett shows how the repercussions for women of this kind of loss extended far into the future. In the case of Violet, now aged nearly 100, it seems to have blighted her whole long life. Remembering *The proper war when all the young lads got killed* (16), she has still *never forgiven* herself for not letting her *young man* make love to her before he left for the Front and was killed.

Aftermath

The signing of the Armistice at 'the eleventh hour of the eleventh day of the eleventh month' in 1918 brought the fighting to an end, and ushered in a new era. Many people rejoiced, but all were faced with the task of coming to terms with everything that had happened during the war years.

Activity
Read Thomas Hardy's poem *'And There Was a Great Calm'* (page 80) and the extract from Vera Brittain's *Testament of Youth* (page 82).

Aftermath

What is the mood of these texts? Is it what you would have expected? How do these writers express their response to the ending of the war?

Discussion

You may have expected to find a sense of excitement, or at least of relief. However, these are almost entirely absent. Instead, the mood is sombre, subdued, depressed, at times even bitter. There is a feeling of exhaustion, or perhaps a failure to feel anything much.

Vera Brittain finds that although some are rejoicing in *a world released from nightmare* (59–60), she is unable to participate. She feels merely numb, and carries on with her work *like a sleeper who is determined to go on dreaming after being told to wake up* (7–8). She moves *Mechanically* and describes herself as *stupidly rigid* (51, 52).

Neither writer includes any sense of victory. According to Vera Brittain, no one says *'We've won the War!'*, just *'The War is over'* (4–5). In Hardy's poem, the war simply stops *One morrow* (23), seemingly at random. The idea of winning has become irrelevant.

Both writers suggest the war was prolonged unnecessarily, because of pride and pugnacity. For Hardy, the question of *Why?* had been ignored (5, 45). He comments through two symbolic voices, the *Spirit of Irony* and the *Spirit of Pity*. Irony, which revels in war and *sneered* (44) and *smirked* at peace because it would *Spoil* the fun (34–35), is clearly the stronger voice; Pity manages only a whisper. Similarly, Vera Brittain believes the war could have *ended rationally... in 1916*, but there was too much *trumpet-blowing*, and a prideful need to fight to the finish in spite of the cost (35–36).

For both writers, there is a sense that peace has come too late. For Hardy, it is too late because any hopes that the world was becoming more civilized – *old hopes that earth was bettering slowly* (21) – have been wiped out; for Vera Brittain, on the more personal level, it is too late for her loved ones who have died, leaving her *a lonely survivor drowning in black waves of memory* (42–43). When she looks back to the beginning of the war, her former life seems *legendary* and unreal (12). She describes having had a premonition that *jubilant celebrations* at the end of the war would be only a *mockery and irony* to those *who have paid with their mourning*

Interpretations

for the others' joy (25–29) – and now she finds she is one of those mourners.

Neither writer expresses any real hope for the future. In his final stanza, Hardy recognizes some *Calm* and *clemency*; but while there is *peace on earth*, there is *silence in the sky*, perhaps suggesting the absence of God (see Notes page 129). Realistically, he remarks that some will recover and *shake off misery*, but others will not. Vera Brittain, too, sees clearly that some people will move on and become *light-hearted and forgetful* (80), while she feels she will have no part in the *brightly lit, alien* future (83).

At this point, it is interesting to turn back to Vera Brittain's diary entry from the beginning of the war (page 16) and the Activity on page 138, and to compare its mood and style with the extract from *Testament of Youth*. Similarly, we can compare Hardy's poem with one he wrote in August 1914, *Men Who March Away* (page 19).

Vera Brittain in her nurse's uniform

Aftermath

Writing 50 years later, Philip Larkin also explores the idea that the war brought about huge and irrevocable changes. In his poem MCMXIV, he aims to capture the mood of the early weeks of the war, but also to show that this era is now very firmly in the past. A certain quality of innocence, like that which we see in the extract from Vera Brittain's diary, as well as in the earnest, idealistic poetry of 1914, has been destroyed and can never be regained.

Activity
Read *MCMXIV* by Philip Larkin (page 92). Discuss or make notes on:
- the ways in which Larkin emphasizes the fact that these scenes are set in the past
- the mood or feeling of the poem
- the overall point of the poem, particularly the final stanza.

Discussion
Larkin's poem creates the effect of looking at old photographs or film footage. Words such as *bleached* (9) and *hazed* (18) suggest these are images of the past that have become faded or blurred, so that they seem distant or not quite real. Describing the men's faces as *archaic* (6) also places them in the distant past. Details such as the coins – *farthings and sovereigns* (11) – which have long become obsolete, and the children who have traditional, patriotic names and are *dark-clothed* (12–13), make the scenes feel unfamiliar and remote.

There is a sense of nostalgia here, for the warmth of summer in the *flowering* countryside, and the idea of a rural way of life that had been constant since the time of the Domesday book (19–20). The *Wide open* pubs seem welcoming (16), and perhaps suggest a light-hearted freedom that is also vulnerable.

The final stanza clearly suggests that the war was a turning point at which an earlier more innocent era came to an end. The war has brought irrevocable changes to lifestyles and expectations, for example in overturning rural traditions or in breaking down the class system that had *differently-dressed servants/ With tiny rooms in huge houses* (22–23).

The men in the photographs look as if they are queuing to enjoy a football or cricket match or a Bank Holiday outing, and expect to return to their tidy gardens. Enormous heartbreak is suggested in the two understated lines: *The thousands of marriages,/ Lasting a little while longer* (30–31).

The people depicted in the poem clearly had no idea what lay in store for them.

Larkin's poem is an effective reminder of the enormous impact of the First World War, and of its haunting irony. It captures the essence of what is represented through the personal testimonies, poetry and imaginative responses in this volume: the general movement from innocent idealism, through needless slaughter and the sacrifice of millions of lives, to a peace tainted with loss, grief and disillusionment.

Essay Questions

1 Read the letter from Roland Leighton to Vera Brittain on page 31. How does Leighton present his experiences here? In your answer you should:
   - compare this extract with your wider reading, saying how typical you think it is of First World War literature
   - look closely at language and style as well as subject matter and themes.

2 Read the poem *The Call* by R.C. Vernède (page 21). How typical is it of First World War poetry? Write a detailed analysis of the poem, in which you compare and contrast it with two other First World War poems of your choice.

3 Read the extract from *The Attack*, in which R.H. Tawney describes taking part in the beginning of the Battle of the Somme (page 36). How does he present the battle and his personal experience of fighting? In your answer you should:
   - compare the extract with your wider reading, saying how typical you think it is of First World War literature
   - consider themes, ideas, language and style.

4 Choose three poems or extracts that present soldiers from different perspectives. Write a detailed comparison of your chosen texts, exploring how the different writers' choices of form, structure and language shape their meanings.

5 Read the extract from *Under Fire* by Henri Barbusse (page 44). What attitudes to war are presented here? In your answer you should:
   - compare the extract with your wider reading, saying how typical you think it is of First World War literature
   - compare and contrast the ways in which different writers' choices of form, structure and language shape meanings.

Essay Questions

6 'The myths that had given value and significance to war were to be stripped away by the poets of 1914–18.' (Bernard Bergonzi)
   - Explore the truth of this statement with close reference to three or four poems from this selection.

7 Read the extract from *In Parenthesis* (page 41) in which David Jones describes soldiers on night manoeuvres on the Western Front. How does he present the men and the landscape here? In your answer you should:
   - compare the extract with your wider reading, saying how typical you think it is of First World War literature
   - compare and contrast the ways in which different writers' choices of form, structure and language shape meanings.

8 Read *To Germany* by Charles Hamilton Sorley (page 30). How typical of First World War literature is the attitude towards the 'enemy' that Sorley presents here? In your answer you should:
   - compare the extract with your wider reading, saying how typical you think it is of First World War literature
   - look closely at language and style as well as subject matter.

9 Read the extract from *Mr Britling Sees It Through*, in which H.G. Wells describes the aftermath of an air raid (page 76).
   - Looking closely at language and style as well as subject matter, explore the ways in which Wells presents Mr Britling's thoughts and feelings about the war.
   - Compare the extract with your wider reading, saying how typical you think it is of First World War literature.

10 Read the extract from *My Heart's Right There* by Florence L. Barclay (page 69). How typical of First World War literature is this portrayal of a woman's response to the war? In your answer you should:
   - explore the extract in relation to your wider reading
   - pay attention to language and style as well as content.

Essay Questions

11 Drawing on the extracts in this collection and any relevant wider reading, write an essay in which you explore the ways in which writers portray the impact of the First World War on the lives of women. In your answer, consider language and style as well as themes and ideas.

12 Read the extract from *Parade's End* by Ford Madox Ford (page 87). How does Ford present the relationships and interactions between men of different ranks in the army here? In your answer you should:
- compare the extract with your wider reading, saying how typical you think it is of First World War literature
- compare and contrast the ways in which writers use different choices of form, structure and language to shape their meanings.

13 Read the poem *Disabled* by Wilfred Owen (page 66). How typical of First World War literature is this portrait of a 'war hero'? In your answer you should:
- compare and contrast the poem with other texts from your wider reading
- look closely at language and style as well as subject matter and themes.

14 Read the texts in the 'Armistice' section (pages 80–86). How do these writers present people's responses to the ending of the war? Are they typical? Looking at language and style as well as themes and ideas, compare the texts with relevant material from your wider reading.

15 Read *MCMXIV* by Philip Larkin (page 92), in which he looks back on the early weeks of the war. How far do you agree with his suggestion that after 1914 there was *Never such innocence again*? Either base your answer on a close study of three texts, or explore the poem in relation to a broader range of your wider reading.

Chronology

Date	Historical, social and political events	Significant literary events and publications
1914	German armies advance in Belgium and against the Russians in Galicia; Britain declares war on 4 August

Defence of the Realm Act (DORA) gives British Government additional powers to control people's behaviour and impose censorship

Battle of the Marne

Recruiting campaigns begin in Britain

Trench warfare begins on the Western Front

First mines are exploded

People opposing the war set up the Union of Democratic Control

Pacifist organization the No-Conscription Fellowship formed

The Christmas Truce: soldiers and officers fraternize with their enemies in No Man's Land | Charles F.G. Masterman, of the War Propaganda Bureau, calls a meeting of well-known writers and asks them to write in support of the war

Songs and Sonnets for England in Wartime

H.G. Wells: *The War That Will End War*

Florence L. Barclay: *My Heart's Right There* |

Chronology

1915	War against Turkey; the Dardanelles campaign and the landings at Gallipoli	Death of Rupert Brooke
		Death of Charles Hamilton Sorley
	German submarine campaign in the Atlantic	
		Robert Nichols: *Invocation*
	First use of gas at the Battle of Ypres, on the Western Front	May Sinclair: *A Journal of Impressions in Belgium*
		Rupert Brooke: *1914 and Other Poems*
	Italy joins the war	
	The Germans inflict further defeats on the Russians, who lose a million soldiers	George Bernard Shaw: *O'Flaherty V.C.*
	The liner *Lusitania* sunk by German submarine	
	Coalition Government takes over from the Liberals; government takes control of munitions factories	
	Zeppelin raids on England begin	
	National Registration Act – all men eligible for military service are registered	
	British and French offensive on the Western Front makes little headway	
	Female Voluntary Aid Detachment (VAD) nurses are first allowed to go to the front line	
	British nurse Edith Cavell executed by the Germans for helping British soldiers to escape	

Chronology

1916	Allied troops are evacuated from Gallipoli	Rose Macaulay: *Non-Combatants and Others*
	Conscription is introduced	Robert Graves: *Over the Brazier*
	Battle of Verdun	
	British troops in Turkey forced to surrender	F.W. Harvey: *A Gloucestershire Lad At Home and Abroad*
	Easter Rising in Dublin – part of a campaign for Irish independence	Charles Hamilton Sorley: *Marlborough and Other Poems*
	Battle of the Somme begins	H.G. Wells: *Mr Britling Sees It Through*
	The Russians lose another million men	Henri Barbusse: *Le Feu* (France)
	First use of tanks	Miles Malleson: *Black 'Ell: A War Play in One Act*
	Lloyd George becomes prime minister	
1917	Submarine warfare a growing threat; ships sail in convoys for protection	Wilfred Owen goes to the Front in France
	Food shortages; bread and other foods are rationed	Edward Thomas (poet) killed in action
	Women's Land Army is formed	Arthur Graeme West (writer) killed in action
	Air raids on east coast towns	Siegfried Sassoon makes his 'Soldier's Declaration', protesting against the handling of the war
	French offensive fails	
	The United States joins the Allies	Wilfred Owen and Siegfried Sassoon meet at Craiglockhart War Hospital, near Edinburgh
	Mutiny in French army	

Chronology

	British offensive – Third Battle of Ypres (Passchendaele) – no progress; terrible conditions in trenches continue	T.E. Hulme (modernist, poet and critic) killed in action
	Bolshevik revolution in Russia	Henri Barbusse: *Under Fire* (English translation of *Le Feu*)
	British victory at Cambrai and small advance	Georges Duhamel: *The New Book of Martyrs* (France)
	Russia pulls out of the war	Ivor Gurney: *Severn and Somme*
		Robert Nichols: *Ardours and Endurances*
		Siegfried Sassoon: *The Old Huntsman and Other Poems*
		Edward Thomas: *Poems*
1918	Women over 30 are given the vote	Isaac Rosenberg killed in action
	Treaty of Brest-Litovsk forces Russians to give up huge amounts of land in the Ukraine, Finland and the Baltic states	Bertrand Russell forbidden to lecture in America and sentenced to 6 months in prison for publishing pacifist article
	Germans begin huge Spring Offensive and advance towards Paris	Wilfred Owen killed in action, one week before the Armistice
	Ministry of Information is created to 'improve morale'	Rebecca West: *The Return of the Soldier*
	Meat rationing introduced	Rupert Brooke: *Collected Poems*
	French and American troops stop the German advance	Ford Madox Ford: *On Heaven, and Poems Written on Active Service*
	Allied counter-offensive begins; Germans now in retreat	

Chronology

	Disintegration of the Austro-Hungarian Empire Education Act raises the school leaving age to 14 Allies on the offensive; Battles of the Marne and Amiens; the Germans are forced to retreat towards the border The war ends with the signing of the Armistice at 11 am on 11 November	Siegfried Sassoon: *The Counter-Attack and Other Poems* Robert Graves: *Fairies and Fusiliers*
1919	US President Woodrow Wilson draws up a 14-point plan to restore stability in Europe; the French consider this too lenient Treaty of Versailles establishes the League of Nations and requires Germany to accept responsibility for the war and pay vast sums in reparations	Arthur Graeme West: *The Diary of a Dead Officer* Charles Hamilton Sorley: *Letters* Richard Aldington: *Images of War* Ivor Gurney: *War's Embers* Herbert Read: *Naked Warriors* Thomas Hardy: *Collected Poems* George Bernard Shaw: *Heartbreak House*

Chronology

1920		Philip Gibbs: *The Realities of War/ Now It Can Be Told* Wilfred Owen: *Poems* (edited by Siegfried Sassoon) Ezra Pound: *Hugh Selwyn Mauberley* Edward Thomas: *Collected Poems*
1921–1925	Irish Free State is established Hyper-inflation and economic crisis in Germany Britain's first Labour government is elected	John Dos Passos: *Three Soldiers* Virginia Woolf: *Jacob's Room* and *Mrs Dalloway* Ford Madox Ford: *Some Do Not…* and *No More Parades* Herbert Read: *In Retreat* T.S. Eliot: *The Waste Land* C.E. Montague: *Disenchantment* and *Fiery Particles* Isaac Rosenberg: *Poems*
1926–1930	The General Strike in protest at miners' pay and working conditions World economic depression	**Memoirs** T.E. Lawrence: *Revolt in the Desert* Edmund Blunden: *Undertones of War* Siegfried Sassoon: *Memoirs of a Fox-Hunting Man* and *Memoirs of an Infantry Officer*

Robert Graves: *Goodbye to All That*

Max Plowman: *A Subaltern on the Somme*

Ernst Junger: *The Storm of Steel* (English translation)

Herbert Read: *Ambush*

Novels

Ford Madox Ford: *A Man Could Stand Up* and *Last Post*

Richard Aldington: *Death of a Hero*

Ernest Hemingway: *A Farewell to Arms*

Erich Maria Remarque: *All Quiet on the Western Front*

Frederic Manning: *Her Privates We (The Middle Parts of Fortune)*

Henry Williamson: *The Patriot's Progress*

Adrienne Thomas: *Katrin Becomes a Soldier*

Helen Zenna Smith: *Not So Quiet: Stepdaughters of War*

Drama

Sean O'Casey: *The Silver Tassie*

R.C. Sherriff: *Journey's End*

Chronology

1931–1935	International conference at Lausanne agrees to suspend Germany's reparation payments, owing to worsening distress in Germany caused by the world depression Adolf Hitler becomes Chancellor of Germany First Nazi concentration camps are built Peace Pledge Union, a pacifist organization, is formed	Aldous Huxley: *Brave New World* Vera Brittain: *Testament of Youth* Guy Chapman: *A Passionate Prodigality* Frank Richards: *Old Soldiers Never Die* T.E. Lawrence: *Seven Pillars of Wisdom*
1936–1940	Spanish Civil War Second World War begins Retreat from Dunkirk Battle of Britain	Deaths of Ivor Gurney and Ford Madox Ford Siegfried Sassoon: *Sherston's Progress* and *The Old Century* Wyndham Lewis: *Blasting and Bombardiering* David Jones: *In Parenthesis* (introduced by T.S. Eliot)
1940s	Japanese bombing of Pearl Harbour; United States joins the war United States drops atomic bombs which destroy Hiroshima and Nagasaki Germany and Japan surrender and the Second World War ends The partition of Germany	Siegfried Sassoon: *The Weald of Youth* and *Siegfried's Journey*

Chronology

	The Cold War – post-war tensions between United States and Russia (USSR) – begins and continues for almost five decades	
1950s	Korean war Britain develops nuclear bomb European Economic Community (EEC) is formed Suez Canal crisis	Henry Williamson: *A Fox Under My Cloak*, *The Golden Virgin*, *Love and the Loveless*, *A Test to Destruction*
1960s	Cuban missile crisis – threat of nuclear war Vietnam War escalates; Americans attack North Vietnam	Death of Siegfried Sassoon Wilfred Owen: *Collected Letters* J.B. Priestley: *Margin Released* Harold Owen: *Journey from Obscurity* Bernard Bergonzi: *Heroes' Twilight* *Oh What a Lovely War* first performed
1970s	Vietnam War ends Britain joins EEC	Jon Stallworthy: *Wilfred Owen: A Biography* Paul Fussell: *The Great War and Modern Memory* Susan Hill: *Strange Meeting*

Chronology

1980s	Falklands War	Death of Robert Graves
		Vera Brittain: *Chronicle of Youth* (war diary)
		Stephen MacDonald: *Not About Heroes*
		Peter Whelan: *The Accrington Pals*
		Lyn Macdonald: *Somme*
		Frank McGuinness: *Observe the Sons of Ulster Marching Towards the Somme*
		Richard Curtis and Ben Elton: *Blackadder Goes Forth* (BBC TV comedy)
1990s	Reunification of Germany Ending of Cold War era The Gulf War	Pat Barker: *Regeneration*, *The Eye in the Door* and *The Ghost Road*
		Sebastian Faulks: *Birdsong*
		Letters from a Lost Generation, edited by Alan Bishop and Mark Bostridge (letters of Vera Brittain, her brother, her fiancé and their friends)

2000s	Terrorist attacks in US, 11 September 2001	Nick Whitby: *To the Green Fields Beyond*
	Wars in Iraq and Afghanistan	Adam Thorpe: *Nineteen Twenty-One*
	Harry Patch, last British survivor of the First World War trenches, dies aged 111	Richard Holmes: *Tommy*
		Voices of Silence: The Alternative Book of First World War Poetry edited by Vivien Noakes
		A Month at the Front: Diary of an Unknown Soldier (Bodleian Library)

Further Reading

Background reading

See the 'Significant literary events and publications' column in the Chronology (page 187) for important works written during and about the war.

General books about the First World War that you will find useful include the following.

Adrian Barlow, *The Great War in British Literature* (Cambridge University Press, 2000)

Bernard Bergonzi, *Heroes' Twilight: A Study of the Literature of the Great War* (3rd edition, Carcanet, 1996)

Paul Fussell, *The Great War and Modern Memory* (Oxford University Press, 1975)

Paul Fussell (ed.), *The Bloody Game: An Anthology of Modern War* (Abacus, 1992)

Dominic Hibberd (ed.), *Poetry of the First World War: A Selection of Critical Essays* (Macmillan, 1981)

Samuel Hynes, *A War Imagined: The First World War and English Culture* (Bodley Head, 1990)

A.J.P. Taylor, *The First World War: An Illustrated History* (Hamish Hamilton, 1963)

You may also wish to read more about individual writers. For example, the following books are about two of the most famous war poets, Wilfred Owen and Siegfried Sassoon.

Max Egremont, *Siegfried Sassoon: A Biography* (Picador, 2005)

Dominic Hibberd, *Wilfred Owen: A New Biography* (Weidenfeld & Nicolson, 2002)

Further Reading

Jon Stallworthy, *Wilfred Owen: A Biography* (Oxford University Press and Chatto & Windus, 1974)
Dennis S.R. Welland, *Wilfred Owen: A Critical Study* (Chatto & Windus, 1960)
Jean Moorcroft Wilson, *Siegfried Sassoon: The Making of a War Poet* (Duckworth, 1998)

Websites

www.bbc.co.uk/history/worldwars/wwone/
Full of useful background information about the First World War, with plenty of illustrations

http://beck.library.emory.edu/greatwar/index.html
Includes e-text editions of poetry collections published in 1914–1918, many of which are unavailable in print, together with an extensive collection of postcards

www.nationalarchives.gov.uk/pathways/firstworldwar/
Includes a broad selection of documents, audio and video material about the First World War

http://www.oucs.ox.ac.uk/ww1lit/
The First World War Poetry Digital Archive, set up by Oxford University, is a freely available, online resource containing over 7000 items of text, images, audio and video for teaching, learning and research

Further Reading

Film

The Battle of the Somme (Geoffrey Malins and John McDowell, 1916, Imperial War Museum) A propaganda film shot to encourage support for the war; available on DVD, or extracts can be found online

All Quiet on the Western Front (Lewis Milestone, 1930) Based on the novel by Erich Maria Remarque

La Grande Illusion (Jean Renoir, 1937)

Paths of Glory (Stanley Kubrick, 1957)

Lawrence of Arabia (David Lean, 1962)

King and Country (Joseph Losey, 1964)

Gallipoli (Peter Weir, 1981)

Blackadder Goes Forth (BBC, 1989)

Regeneration (Gillies Mackinnon, 1997) Based on the novel by Pat Barker

The First World War (Jonathan Lewis, 2004) 10-part series, available on DVD

The Somme (Carl Hindmarch, 2005) Channel 4 documentary; can be viewed online